LATINO PLACEMAKING
AND PLANNING

Latinx Pop Culture

SERIES EDITORS

Frederick Luis Aldama and Arturo J. Aldama

LATINO PLACEMAKING AND PLANNING

Cultural Resilience and Strategies for Reurbanization

Jesus J. Lara

THE UNIVERSITY OF
ARIZONA PRESS
TUCSON

The University of Arizona Press
www.uapress.arizona.edu

© 2018 by The Arizona Board of Regents
All rights reserved. Published 2018

ISBN-13: 978-0-8165-3709-9 (paper)

Cover design by Leigh McDonald
Cover photo: *Bagley & Sainte Anne* by Lian Chang

All photos and graphic content are the author's unless otherwise noted. All GIS maps were created with the assistance of Yujin Park.

Library of Congress Cataloging-in-Publication Data are available at the Library of Congress.

Printed in the United States of America
♾ This paper meets the requirements of ANSI/NISO Z39.48-1992 (Permanence of Paper).

CONTENTS

ILLUSTRATIONS

Figures

Tables

ACKNOWLEDGMENTS

I am grateful for the assistance and support provided by numerous individuals that made this book possible. Thanks to the editors of the Latinx Pop Culture series, Professors Frederick L. Aldama and Arturo J. Aldama, for their unconditional support on this project. To the University of Arizona Press, for considering this a viable project. To the Latinx community leaders, business owners, and residents who contributed during the interview and documentation process of the different case studies in cities across the country. Finally, to the reviewers who provided suggestions that helped improve the final text.

LATINO PLACEMAKING AND PLANNING

INTRODUCTION

Latino Americans are currently the second-largest ethnic group within the United States. By the year 2050 they are projected to number nearly 133 million, or approximately one-third of the country's total population. As the urban component of this population increases, the increased need for resources to support it will generate new cultural and economic stresses.

This book attempts to define, analyze, and evaluate the role of *placemaking* with respect to Latino communities in the context of contemporary urban planning, policy, and design practices. Selected cases studies are employed to examine how Latinos contribute to the phenomenon of urban revitalization through the (re) appropriation of physical space for their own use and the consequent transformation of what were previously economically downtrodden areas into vibrant commercial and residential centers. These case studies also highlight the approaches urban designers, public policy makers, academics, and business owners use within Latino communities to revitalize obsolete and underutilized retail corridors and deteriorating urban and suburban neighborhoods while bringing about improvements in both the economic and overall quality of life.

The analysis here expands upon the growing body of literature concerned with the needs and impacts of relatively new Latino communities in relation to the established environment and its development. Specifically: when Latino immigrants establish new "places" in urban centers across the country, how do those places change, what are the qualities and conditions that make those places unique, and what are the implications for an increasingly culturally and demographically diverse urban landscape? These are some of the questions this book seeks to answer through an analysis and understanding of the contemporary urban condition and, particularly, its distinct Latino dimension.

The book presents a series of case studies from cities throughout the United States where Latinos have had a positive impact in placemaking. The analysis, synthesis, and documentation of the spatial and visual landscape are key components of these studies. When immigrants come to the United States they carry with them cultural traits and characteristics that influence how they use public spaces, conduct their social lives, and create dynamic urban spaces. Besides forming a basis to evaluate placemaking in Latino communities, the case studies demonstrate Latino contributions to the urban revitalization process through the (re)appropriation of space and its consequent use in a culturally specific manner. In urban centers across the country cultural entrepreneurs and ethnic minorities are giving new meaning to abandoned urban landscapes once characterized by derelict strip malls and deteriorating urban and suburban residential neighborhoods, while also contributing to the economic development in those areas. Immigrant businesses often grow out of underserved markets, generally starting as microenterprises: that is, businesses with low start-up costs and low economies of scale. These enterprises tend to be adept at providing goods and services in neighborhoods where demand is uncertain.

Case studies, an important component of this research, expand the information gained from a general literature review and highlight some of the most innovative strategies in placemaking and design that Latino communities have experienced. The selected case studies are by no means the only relevant work worth consideration, but as Robert Yin suggests, there is a specific value in case studies in their potential to "retain holistic and meaningful characteristics of real-life events" (Yin 1994). Moreover, according to Marc Francis (1999), the case study in the design and planning professions is a highly appropriate and valuable tool simply because most of the research and practice in these fields is already based to some extent on case study methodology. The studies examined here are used to demonstrate the resiliency of the Latino community and its potential for placemaking with the intent of identifying the "edge" of innovation in sustainable revitalization-oriented projects.

The case studies emerged from the author's own engagement with various communities, and each reveals particular aspects of the social, economic, and cultural resilience in ethnic and immigrant communities through studies of their entrepreneurial practices. Each case study is organized into four sections. First, a "Context and Background" section provides an overview of the physical transformation and adaptation of the corridors and the research methodology. Second, "Demographic Trends and Impacts" covers demographic changes and their social, cultural, and economic ramifications. Third, "Economic Trends and Impacts" analyzes trends in purchasing power, business growth, and overall commercial development, highlighting the important role of Latino businesses in the community. Finally, "Summary and Implications for Future Planning" describes how Latinos are transforming the cultural and economic landscape in derelict and abandoned urban districts and provides recommendations that serve as a call to action to city governments, planners, social groups, and community organizations. With a better understanding of the processes and transformations that these commercial corridors are experiencing, policy makers, civic leaders, urban planners, and designers can more effectively revitalize urban centers and facilitate healthier Latino communities.

The study of the benefits of social networks and economic revitalization in immigrant neighborhoods required a combination of research methods. The applied methodology involved principally qualitative data. Research involved two stages. First, an inventory was made of the service provider businesses owned by Latinos or geared specifically toward this ethnic community in each case study area. This was followed by an analysis of the study area's visual landscape by identifying urban forms and patterns. The second stage of research included informal interviews with local business owners and their customers, stakeholders, local nonprofit organization officials, and residents. Field data on Latino business types, services provided, and locations within each corridor was collected and compared with spatial patterns along the length of each of the studied corridors, the focus being on sociocultural patterns of Latino communities in each of the study areas. Particularly important information from secondary sources was acquired using qualitative ethnographic techniques such as field observation, as well as from photo and video documentation.

Data was collected over a three-year period, during which time random site visits involved street observation, mapping, photo documentation, and document analysis. Observations included but were not limited to patterns and use of city blocks, building typology, recreational facilities, and formal and informal activity settings.

Secondary sources of information included a variety of documents and reports from the public domain as well as from nonprofit organizations. Material from newspapers and journals (both print and online), as well as census and economic and employment data, was collected and analyzed.

The questions asked during the informal interviews included the following: Why did you choose to come to this city over any other city in the United States? What is attractive about this city/neighborhood in which you live? Is the Latino community helpful here? Is the Latino community strong here? Are there many places for Latinos to get together and socialize? Can one easily find authentic Latino food and groceries here?

The research and analysis here ideally will provide urban planners and designers, policy makers, landscape architects and students of landscape architecture, and academics with an interdisciplinary perspective on global and local challenges faced by immigrant communities in urbanized areas. A further goal has been to identify the role Latino migrants are playing in the revitalization or "reconstruction" of urban communities throughout the United States. Relevant information and insights have been provided that can potentially aid designers and policy decision makers alike. A better understanding of the needs of and challenges facing the Latino community today is needed to guarantee that future urban planning and design practices work to best serve this population.

Much of the inspiration for this book comes from a special edition of the *Journal of Urbanism* that focused on the topic of Latino urbanism, of which I was the guest editor and contributor, as well from an Ohio State University course I taught, "Latino Urbanism and the Reinvention of the American City," which examines Latino communities and diversity themes in a variety of contexts, from cultural and historical debates over the use of major public spaces to a wide range of more contemporary issues.

It is my intent that this book will expand the dialogue, extend challenges, and disseminate information about emerging approaches concerning the management of urban environments in relation to the Latino community. Particular stress has been placed on the interrelationship of the notions of place and identity as an approach for retrofitting cities and neighborhoods.

The book's contents are structured into the following four chapters that explore the theme of defining cultural urban formation and reurbanization strategies with Latino urbanism.

Chapter 1: Emerging New Urban Geographies

The initial chapter provides an overview and analysis of the shifting economic and demographic trends that characterize Latinos in this country. Such trends should be of interest to any and all who are concerned with the future of urban America or with the issue of equity in American society. The chapter stresses that as the size and complexity of the U.S. Latino population increase, so does its influence on America's urban space, its politics, and its culture. The focus is on why those who help plan and shape our physical environment should be concerned with the characteristics of Latino urban populations, while, in turn, those concerned with Latino urban populations should be interested in the urban landscape.

Chapter 2: The Power of Place and Neighborhood Selection

Chapter 2 examines the process of "placemaking" in Latino neighborhoods. This involves (1) a review of current literature on the concept; (2) an examination of its role and application in Latino urbanism; and (3) an assessment of its effects on the development and evolution of Latino neighborhoods in the United States. More specifically, placemaking is analyzed in terms of how it has impacted urban environments culturally and contributed to their sociocultural infrastructure and support networks. Understanding placemaking is crucial to understanding why and how Latino neighborhoods develop in large urban areas and whether or not they continue to thrive.

Chapter 3: Unveiling Latino Urbanism Case Studies

Chapter 3 examines the development of ethnic entrepreneurship, identifying the signs of socioeconomic revitalization that can appear in the urban landscape of new Latino immigrant communities. Case studies of commercial corridors revitalized by Latinos from selected cities across the country are analyzed: in Phoenix, Arizona; Detroit,

Michigan; Columbus, Ohio; and Indianapolis, Indiana. The types of projects examined are intentionally diverse and encompass a wide range of activities of varying scales. In order to contextualize the impact that Latinos have had on the selected cities, four key areas of analysis are undertaken: (1) an exploration of the physical transformations and economic changes experienced by Latinos in the communities studied; (2) detailed examination of neighborhood selection criteria, highlighting the important roles that Latino businesses play in the community; (3) an analysis of the presence and level of support afforded by social networks; and (4) a detailed review of the physical and typological characteristics of urban demographic composition and neighborhood structure, providing a synthesis of lessons learned from each case study.

Chapter 4: Lessons and Recommendations for Re-urbanizing the City

This final chapter explains the implications for planning and design from the findings of the case studies in selected U.S. cities, including potential lessons for other emerging immigrant destinations in this country. An overview of the steps that planners and policy makers can take is offered. The principal issues addressed include appropriate responses to an urban population's increasing levels of diversity and consequently changing demands on infrastructure, evaluation of the processes and mechanisms that contribute to ethnocultural alienation within Latino neighborhoods, and the establishment of safeguards where Latino economic and cultural assets are protected in the course of any revitalization efforts. The chapter includes a series of guidelines and recommendations for establishing enabling systems in planning and design policy that reflect the linkages between immigration and the physical environment in terms of three factors: population growth, neighborhood revitalization, and economic development.

Chapter 1

EMERGING NEW URBAN GEOGRAPHIES

Latino Americans represent the fastest-growing ethnic group in the United States, one with rapidly increasing cultural, economic, and political impacts on American society. Studies indicate that the U.S. Latino population is not only growing faster and is younger in complexion than the U.S. population overall, but also is increasingly educated, employed, connected, entrepreneurial, and upwardly mobile in terms of income as well as consumption (Eisenach 2016). Latinos have made enormous contributions in several areas. Not only are Latinos prominent within the entertainment and communications industries, but they now occupy important positions within the business community and have fielded U.S. presidential candidates. In spite of these achievements, it is important not to mistake Latinos as any sort of monolithic group. Region and country of origin often determine many cultural characteristics. Whereas a Mexican heritage distinguishes the majority of Latinos in America overall, those of Puerto Rican descent easily outnumber all other Latino populations in New York City. All Latino neighborhoods further feature a mixture of recent immigrants and the native born, as well as second- and third-generation Americans. Some residents speak only Spanish; some speak only English; and some are bilingual. Some are working or lower class, some middle class, and some (particularly in South Florida) are members of the wealthiest classes.

The Pew Research Center has aptly termed the American Latino community "an awakened giant" (Taylor et al. 2012). Demographic evidence substantiating this can be found in the 2013 edition of the U.S. Census Bureau's *American FactFinder*, where (officially) the total Latino population, as of July 2014, is said to be 55 million. Moreover, by 2009 Latinos had already constituted 20 percent of all elementary and high school students in the United States, with over a million Latinos aged eighteen or older possessing advanced degrees. Economically, receipts generated by Latino-owned businesses reached $350.7 billion in 2007, representing an astonishing 55.5 percent increase from the 2002 figure. In political terms, approximately 9.7 million Latino citizens voted in the 2008 U.S. presidential election, up 2 million from the 2004 poll count. Moreover, the *percentage* of registered Latino voters balloting rose from 47 to 50 percent between these two elections. With two Latino Americans contending for presidential office in 2012, this number is expected to rise further.

Overall, between April of 2000 and April of 2010, the Latino population of the United States increased 43 percent, the largest percentage gain of any minority group subject to statistical grouping. Whereas in 2010 Latinos constituted 17 percent of the U.S. population, it is projected that by 2060 Latinos will number approximately 128.8 million, or 31 percent of the nation's total population. This shift in the demographic landscape of the United States (which has been gaining steam for at least the past thirty years) is visible throughout the country, whether in small rural farm communities or large metropolitan urban centers.

As Latino populations grow in cities and towns across America, the need for resources to support them creates new economic and cultural stresses that are manifested at the national scale in both urban and rural settings. The discussion included in this chapter relates to these emerging new urban geographies and explores the benefits, challenges, and opportunities with which Latino American culture is presented. Key factors that highlight the new urban geographies of the Latino population across the country include (1) population growth and shifting demographics, (2) the power of the Latino market, (3) increased buying power, and (4) trends in labor force characteristics and voting.

Population Growth and Shifting Demographics

Immigration was one of the principal factors that shaped the twentieth-century American metropolis, and it continues as a driving force behind many of the most important changes occurring in U.S. cities today. It is a social force that has profound economic, social, and physical impacts (Bernstein 2005; Lara 2012a; Myers 1999). For the U.S. Latino population, immigration has been one of the most significant factors contributing to its growth. According to the U.S. Census Bureau, between 1980 and 2012 the Latino population of the United States grew from 14.6 million to 53 million, making it the second-largest racial/ethnic group in the country behind white Americans, numbering approximately 198 million, but above African Americans, numbering approximately 40 million (Malavé and Giordani 2014). The growth of the Latino population was accompanied by its dissemination to new destinations across the country.

The increasing Latino complexion of the population is one of several demographic trends within the United States. In 2008 the U.S. Census Bureau projected that by midcentury the nation will be not only more racially and ethnically diverse, but also much older. According to these estimates, "minorities" (now roughly a third of the U.S. population) will become the "majority" by 2042, and by 2050 the nation's population will actually be 54 percent "minorities." Also in 2050, the minority component of the country's child population is projected to reach 62 percent versus the current 44 percent, and it is estimated that 39 percent of all children will be Latino (versus 22 percent in 2008), while only 38 percent will be single-race, non-Latino white (versus 56 percent in 2008) (U.S. Census Bureau 2012). Further, by 2030 (a time by which all "baby boomers" will be sixty-five years or older), the number of Americans over sixty-five will climb to 88.5 million, or more than twice the number (38.7 million) for 2008 (U.S. Census Bureau 2012). Therefore, increased diversity of the U.S. population will be accompanied by its graying. It should be noted, however, that the primary future driver for Latino population growth will be births among Latinos residing in the United States rather than immigration, whose contribution to this sector's growth continues to decline (Malavé and Giordani 2014).

When looking at Latino demographics separately, the most important characteristics whose evaluation provides insight are overall population growth, geographical distribution of that growth, and change in percentage composition of the total population. As already stated, the Latino population of the United States as of July 2012 was estimated at 53 million. This represents 17 percent of the nation's entire population and establishes Latinos as the nation's largest ethnic or racial minority (U.S. Census Bureau 2011). The nation's Latino population, which stood at 35.3 million in 2000, rose 43 percent in a decade, or more than four times the 10 percent growth of the population at large. Moreover, the rise in the Latino population accounted for more than half of the nation's growth (56 percent) between 2000 and 2010 (Cohen, Passel, and Lopez 2011).

The Latino presence in the United States is not limited to what were considered "historical" or "traditional" destinations ten to fifteen years ago, but encompasses essentially the entire nation. Nor are foreign-born populations, including Latinos, confined to inner-city neighborhoods and downtown areas as immigrants often were in the past; rather, they now often choose to reside in the suburbs—places that have historically been viewed as predominantly enclaves of white and upper-middle-class families (Agius 2012; Flippen 2012; Singer, Hardwick, and Brettel 2008; Zúñiga and Hernández-León 2005).

The greater geographical distribution of Latinos across the United States became noticeable in the 1990s and early years of the twenty-first century when many Latino immigrants bypassed such traditional gateways as New York, Chicago, Los Angeles, and Miami for the more novel destinations of Atlanta, Georgia; Charlotte, North Carolina; Las Vegas, Nevada; Portland, Oregon; and Minneapolis, Minnesota, to cite a few (Agius 2012; Goździak and Martin 2005; Singer, Hardwick, and Brettel 2008; Zúñiga and Hernández-León 2005). The new relocation opportunities were made possible by an improved employment outlook accompanying the economic boom that occurred in the high tech and financial services sectors of the U.S. economy during this period and was not confined to the traditional gateway cities. Although California, Texas, New York, Florida, and Illinois continued to be routine immigrant destinations, five other states rivaled them in the growth of their own Latino populations: Alabama, South Carolina, Tennessee, Kentucky, and South Dakota (Malavé and Giordani 2014). According to the 2010 Census Briefs, in 2010 41 percent of all Latinos lived in the West and 36 percent lived in the South (U.S. Census Bureau 2011), for a total of more than three-quarters of the entire group's population. The Northeast and Midwest accounted for only 14 percent and 9 percent, respectively, of the same total. Latinos accounted for 29 percent of the total population in the West, the only region in which Latinos exceeded the national level of 16 percent. The Latino population grew in every region between 2000 and 2010, but most significantly in the South and Midwest. The Latino population of the South grew 57 percent, a rate four times that of the overall population (14 percent). Significant growth also occurred in the Midwest, where Latino numbers rose by 49 percent, or more than twelve times the growth rate for the overall population (4 percent). Latino growth rates in other parts of the country were lower, but in all instances still exceeded that of either the regional or national overall increase. The Northeast's Latino population grew by 33 percent, or ten times that of the general population (3 percent) (U.S. Census Bureau 2011).

At a more local level, Latino populations in 912 of 3,143 U.S. counties at least doubled between 2000 and 2010. Whereas in 1990, 90 percent of the total U.S. population lived in the 220 counties with at least ten thousand Latino residents, by 2000 only 87 percent did; and by 2007 only 84 percent (Fry 2008). Among the 469 counties in 2010 with at least ten thousand Latino residents, the five fastest-growing were all in the South or Midwest: Luzerne, Pennsylvania (479 percent increase); Henry, Georgia (339 percent); Kendall, Illinois (338 percent); Douglas, Georgia (321 percent); and Shelby, Alabama (297 percent). More than two-thirds (69 percent) of all counties experienced percentage increases between 2000 and 2010 higher than the 43 percent figure for the nation overall (U.S. Census Bureau 2011).

In summary, Latinos are not only increasing in numbers but are moving to areas that historically have had more limited immigration experience, such as in the South and Midwest. This is reflected in the extraordinary changes in county populations cited above. There is little evidence such trends will decelerate in either rural or urban areas, or that the accompanying changes in the social, cultural, and economic landscape they bring about will as well.

Power of the Latino Market

The sheer enhanced demographics of the Latino population now make the U.S. economy both sensitive and vulnerable to social and cultural shifts within its second-largest ethnic grouping. Not only do Latinos constitute America's largest single minority, but they are its fastest-growing one, as well as having the youngest population. Moreover, the Latino entrepreneurial spirit is distinct. All of these characteristics contribute toward ethnic plurality with respect to business practices used in the Latino community and marketing

Percent Change in Hispanic and Latino Population, 2000 - 2010

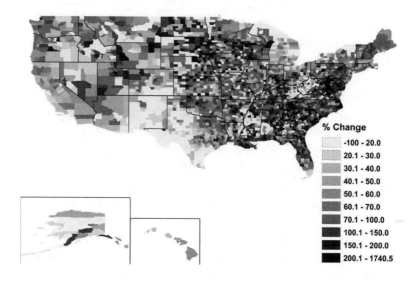

% Change
- -100 - 20.0
- 20.1 - 30.0
- 30.1 - 40.0
- 40.1 - 50.0
- 50.1 - 60.0
- 60.1 - 70.0
- 70.1 - 100.0
- 100.1 - 150.0
- 150.1 - 200.0
- 200.1 - 1740.5

Percent of Hispanic and Latino Population by County in 2000

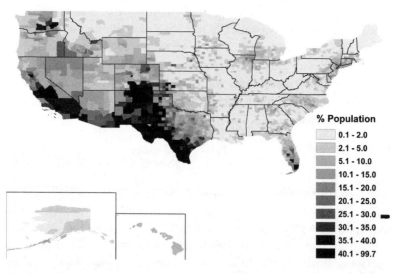

% Population
- 0.1 - 2.0
- 2.1 - 5.0
- 5.1 - 10.0
- 10.1 - 15.0
- 15.1 - 20.0
- 20.1 - 25.0
- 25.1 - 30.0
- 30.1 - 35.0
- 35.1 - 40.0
- 40.1 - 99.7

Figure 1. Latino population change across the country. In some counties in the Midwest the Latino population grew 500 to 700 percent. The Latino population is expected to grow by 29.2 percent and make up 53.3 percent of the total population growth by 2050. Source: *American FactFinder* (U.S. Census Bureau).

Percent Change in Hispanic and Latino Population, 2000 - 2014

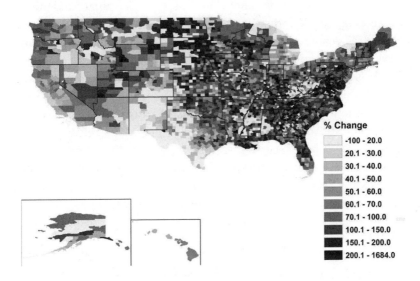

% Change

	-100 - 20.0
	20.1 - 30.0
	30.1 - 40.0
	40.1 - 50.0
	50.1 - 60.0
	60.1 - 70.0
	70.1 - 100.0
	100.1 - 150.0
	150.1 - 200.0
	200.1 - 1684.0

Percent of Hispanic and Latino Population by County in 2014

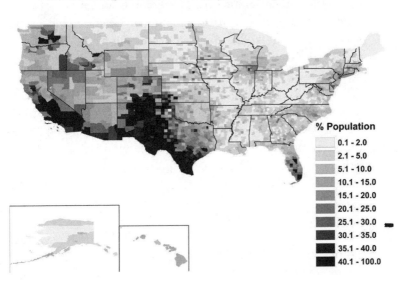

% Population

	0.1 - 2.0
	2.1 - 5.0
	5.1 - 10.0
	10.1 - 15.0
	15.1 - 20.0
	20.1 - 25.0
	25.1 - 30.0
	30.1 - 35.0
	35.1 - 40.0
	40.1 - 100.0

techniques directed toward them. This ethnic plurality has already been reflected in the commercial spheres of urban areas with the largest Latino populations and will only spread as younger and more widely geographically distributed Latino centers develop. The success of the U.S. economy necessarily will become increasingly dependent on the Latino market (Nielsen Company 2012).

High birth rates, continued immigration, and increased entrepreneurship contributed to a staggering $1.3 trillion valuation of the U.S. Latino market in 2015. If this valuation was translated into the gross domestic product (GDP) of a single country, it would represent the fourteenth largest economy in the world, one larger than that of either Spain or Mexico and approximately equivalent to the GDP of the Russian Federations (Eisenach 2016). In their study *The State of the Hispanic Consumer*, the Nielsen Company (2012) identified six characteristics of this market that have promoted its growth and will continue to do so:

1. *Latinos are a fundamental component of business success, not a passing niche on the sidelines.* One misconception from which many U.S. companies suffer is the stereotype of Latinos as a relatively economically deprived, marginally acculturated group possessing little credit. Such misconceptions prevent businesses from capitalizing on the phenomenon of the extraordinary wealth creation taking place within the Latino community (Castro 2013). The 2010 U.S. Census revealed that those Latino households earning $100,000 or more grew from 7 percent to 17 percent of the total Latino population from 2002 through 2009. Moreover, during the past decade, while total U.S. households with incomes exceeding $100,000 grew only 87 percent, Latino households in that category rose 221 percent, consequently increasing the Latino share of all households earning $100,000 or more from 3.7 percent to 6.5 percent.

2. *Rapid Latino population growth will persist, even if immigration is completely halted.* The 2014 *American FactFinder* showed the Latino population to be 55 million. Between July 2011 and July 2012 alone, Latino numbers increased 1.1 million, constituting almost half of the total 2.3 million increase in the U.S. population during that period. Moreover, every month at least fifty thousand

young Latinos reach the statistically and economically significant age of eighteen. Consequently, the marketing departments of many American businesses are realizing that they ignore these Latino demographics in their advertising campaigns only at their own peril (Castro 2013; Nielsen Company 2012).

3. *Latinos have amassed significant buying power.* As stated, the Latino portion of the U.S. economy was estimated at $1.3 trillion in 2013. There are three million Latino-owned businesses in the United States, businesses that are projected to grow an additional 41.8 percent (or three times the faster than the number of businesses overall) to 4.3 million in the next six years.

4. *Latinos are the largest immigrant group to exhibit significant cultural sustainability and are not disappearing into the American melting pot.* There are sixteen states with a half million or more Latinos, and in all of these states their overall household incomes are trending upward. Moreover, more Latinos are attending college than ever before, suggesting further increases in income levels. Since Latinos are a much younger demographic, averaging approximately ten years younger than the overall population, their impact on the housing market is expected to be disproportional as well (Acosta 2013).

5. *Latino technology and media use do not mirror the general market but have distinct patterns owing to language, culture, and ownership dynamics.* U.S. Latinos have been early adopters of mobile technology. Seventy-four percent of Latino mobile users are between the ages of eighteen and forty-four and spend over twenty hours per week using social media. Among the 52 percent of Latinos with access to online computer services, 70 percent prefer to surf the web in English, 17 percent prefer Spanish, and 13 percent do not have any language preference (Nielsen Company 2012).

6. *Latinos exhibit distinct product consumption patterns and are not buying in ways that are the same as the total market.* The number of U.S. Latinos accessing online computer services increased from 29 million to 39 million between 2009 and 2014. Furthermore, Spanish is now the third most popularly used language on the web (Nielsen Company 2012). Advertising specific to the Latino community exceeds $5 billion annually, with

companies like Procter & Gamble, McDonald's, AT&T, Verizon, Toyota, General Mills, and General Motors now typically spending tens to hundreds of millions of dollars individually (Nielsen Company 2012). Such advertising is growing at four times the rate for the industry overall and outpaces that targeted for any other ethnic group. In 2011 alone there was an 11 percent increase in advertising expenditures directed to the Latino market, a market where 51 percent of the recipients prefer such advertising in Spanish as opposed to English (Nielsen Company 2012).

These six key points underscore that Latinos are fast becoming preeminent drivers of growth and likely trendsetters in the marketplace given their youth, sheer numbers, educational advances, and increased spending capacity.

Latino immigrants are often characterized by the entrepreneurial spirit and resiliency necessary for success in the marketplace. Research undertaken by the Carnegie Endowment for International Peace on immigrant entrepreneurs found that one of the reasons that neighborhood revitalizations driven by ethnic minorities are successful is that immigrants are frequently by nature entrepreneurial (Aronson 1997). The same study indicates that every census between 1890 and 1990 has shown that immigrants were significantly more likely to be self-employed than were native-born Americans. In "Immigrant Entrepreneurs," David Aronson argues that this is largely attributable to the fact that members of a household who choose to immigrate abroad often have those characteristics—such as dynamic risk-taking—associated with entrepreneurship. Indeed, evidence from many different cities has shown that immigrants have played significant roles in economic revitalization over the last three decades (Aronson 1997).

Examples abound of how entire neighborhoods and city districts have been revitalized by Latino immigrants. The Mexicans of the Broadway District in Downtown Los Angeles, the Dominicans of Washington Heights in New York, the Cubans of Miami's Little Havana, and, most recently, the Mexicans of Mexicantown in Detroit and the Sullivant and Morse Corridors in Columbus, Ohio, have all turned ailing neighborhoods around. In most of these cases the benefits of these new and viable commercial districts include (1) contributions to economic growth and prospects for continued development; and (2) promotion of a sense of place, identity, and placemaking.

In all of the major cities across the country with significant Latino populations, Latinos have been reconfiguring the sociocultural and economic meaning of urban life (Diaz 2005), as well as disproportionately influencing economic growth and development, a trend that is expected to continue for at least the next quarter century (Suro 2002). The rise in Latino population and consequent economic power has also impacted the manner in which retail and service businesses operate, a process that continues to evolve as Latino economic participation and purchasing power increases further. As noted by the Selig Center for Economic Growth, demographics favor continued and heightened purchasing power for Latinos because the relative youth of this population means it is contributing *new* members to the workforce at much higher rates than is the general population (Humphreys 2013). A 2012 survey by the same center revealed that 33.8 percent of the Latino population is less than eighteen years old versus 21.3 percent of the non-Latino population. Another study, undertaken by Latino Trending, indicates that the number of Latino business owners has significantly increased in response to the increased demands for particular ethnic goods and services of their population group (Tornoe 2004), while non-Latino grocers nationwide are looking at ways to increase sales by adding more ethnic foods to store shelves (McTaggart 2004). In 2006 the U.S. Census Bureau released data indicating commercial enterprises owned by Latinos grew by 31 percent between 1997 and 2002, a rate more than triple the 10 percent rise in such enterprises overall (Humphreys 2013). In 2007 the number of Latino-owned businesses was 2.23 million, up 43.6 percent from 2002. The commensurate rise in the revenues of these businesses to $350.7 billion was an even higher 58 percent. The changing demographics underlying these significant increases are supplemented by the support of the Latino Chamber of Commerce and local nonprofit organizations for the development of new Latino enterprises. Entrepreneurial immigrants hoping for an improved economic life in the United States and national chain stores seeking to increase revenues have been the groups to capitalize most on the growing Latino consumer market.

Many examples of success among entrepreneurial immigrants can be found in the study areas discussed in chapter 3, particularly groceries and restaurants. Such successful new establishments include Food City and Rancho Market in Phoenix; La Mexicana, La Fiesta Market, and La Piedad in Detroit; and La Michoacana and La Plaza Tapatia in Columbus. Their success is largely attributable to catering specifically to the needs of the Latino community through the use of bilingual staff, advertising, and establishment signage, all of which are essential in attracting customers with limited English language skills.

The proliferation of independently owned Latino businesses is not a regional phenomenon, but rather one taking place throughout the United States: across the Sunbelt region, within the South, and even in the Midwest, where Latinos are becoming the largest ethnic minority. According to the Mexican American Association of Grocers (MAGA), those independent businesses that have been most successful understand the culture and economics of the communities in which they operate. In turn, immigrants tend to be loyal consumers, retaining the custom of buying from markets in their local villages (Tornoe 2005). When immigrants continue this tradition in their adopted homeland, they tend to shop almost exclusively in neighborhood markets, contributing to both the success of minority-owned businesses and to the vitality of the neighborhoods in question. These trends further raise Latino visibility, as the new businesses (whether independent or part of national chains) feature the Spanish language in their establishments' signs and advertising.

Increased Buying Power

As noted by the Selig Center for Economic Growth, the increase in Latino population has been accompanied by an increase in this population's purchasing power. Purchasing power (also termed "disposable income") is defined as total personal income available for spending on goods and services after taxes. State-by-state projections of this statistic can be reflected in terms of market size, growth rate, and market share (Humphreys 2013). According to the Selig Center (Humphreys 2013), over the twenty-nine-year period between 1990 and 2018, Latino purchasing power within the United States will rise dramatically. Between 1990 and 2000 the aggregate figure rose from $210 billion to $491 billion, then to $1 trillion in 2010, and to $1.2 trillion in 2013. The projected figure for 2018 is $1.6 trillion. This study further indicates spending patterns among Latinos distinct from the population at large. Latinos proportionately outspent non-Latino whites and African Americans with respect to groceries (particularly meat, fresh fruit, and vegetables), apparel and footwear, phone service, and used vehicles in 2013 (Humphreys 2013). Latinos also spend proportionately more on clothing for all children under the age of two, and for female children between the ages of two and fifteen. A survey by Latino Trending indicates that much of the increase in Latino-owned businesses can be attributed to those businesses addressing these distinct buying patterns (Tornoe 2004). Similarly, national grocery chains are now looking at ways to increase sales by adding more ethnic foods to their shelves (McTaggart 2004).

Statistical analysis easily discredits stereotypes of the U.S. Latino population as poor, uneducated, lacking in upward mobility, and as merely laborers or service workers of the informal economy. Rather, in 2013 over one in three Latinos (37 percent) fell within the "upscale" economic stratification, enjoying annual incomes between $50,000 and $100,000 and responsible for $500 million of the $1.3 trillion that Latinos received in income that year (Gil-Valletta 2013). *The Harvard Business Review* cited five reasons why this market cannot be ignored:

- The upscale segment is projected to double in size by 2050, encompassing 35 million households.
- The segment is young and vibrant. While white baby boomers age, upscale Latinos will remain relatively young and living in growing households. Latinos, on average, are thirty-three years of age versus thirty-nine years for the general population, which implies more active lifestyles and younger families.
- The segment is relatively localized, with 60 percent of its members residing in the Southwest and Pacific regions of the United States, where businesses ignore the consequent economic clout at their own peril.
- Upscale Latinos are purchasing more, spending more per trip on vacations and on health and beauty items than do upscale whites.
- The segment is both entrepreneurial and educated. Between 2010 and 2011 alone Latino college enrollment

rose 15 percent. Moreover, one-half million Latino homes include a household member who owns their own business (Gill 2013; New America Alliance Institute 2014).

Any examination of birth rates, purchasing power, and statistics related to Latino gender tends to show the disproportionate influence of Latino women versus men on the U.S. economy. According to the Nielsen Company study previously cited (2012), Latino women are responsible for most of their household's economic decisions. Their influence on the overall economy can only increase, as these women are projected to constitute 30 percent of the total female population by 2060, while the figure for the non-Latino white female population is expected to drop to 43 percent (Nielsen Company 2012). Latinas are becoming more educated, tech savvy, and professionally connected, all of which gives them more control over their careers and the ability to challenge the traditional dynamics of the Latino household. That 86 percent of Latino women are said to be at the helm of their households' purchasing decisions is yet another indication of their disproportionate influence (Armas, McCaskill, and Roussell 2017).

Latino consumers have a tendency to favor brand names, as evidenced by fashion footwear sales, where between June 2012 and May 2013 Latino women accounted for $3.3 billion, or 18 percent, of the total women's fashion footwear market (NPD Group 2013). Although it may come as a revelation to some, many luxury brands have targeted the upscale Latino market. Brands that have partnered with the U.S. Latino Chamber of Commerce (USHCC) include BMW, Visa Inc., Gucci Timepieces and Jewelry, and Ralph Lauren. Furthermore, advertising agencies specializing in Spanish advertisements for publications such as *Vanidades*, *People en Español*, and *Latina* have developed partnerships with retailers such as Macy's, organized promotions involving celebrities, and participated in what are considered posher or more exclusive Latino events (Castro 2013; Gil 2013). The Latino market, through its growing purchasing power, is already part of the "consumer base" of many luxury brands.

Another facet of the U.S. economy in which Latinos are having an increasing impact is real estate. A report by the National Association of Latino Real Estate Professionals (Calderon and Becerra 2016) found the following: (1) Latinos accounted for 355,000 (51 percent) of the total net increase of 693,000 homeowner households in the United States during 2012; (2) home ownership for Latinos grew from 4.2 million households in 2000 to 6.7 million in 2012, a 58 percent increase, compared to a mere 5 percent increase for the rest of the U.S. population; (3) Latinos are expected to account for 40 percent (5 million) of the estimated 12 million to 14 million net new households within the next decade; and (4) more than one million Latino households were formed in 2012, compared to an actual decrease of 704,000 households among whites (Acosta 2013). The study also noted the importance of home ownership among Latino families. It found that approximately 56 percent of those interviewed stated that their principal motivation for home ownership was how it symbolized success or achievement as part of the "American dream." Conversely, less than a third of all non-Latinos held the same view. The study concluded that Latino homebuyers are poised to drive the residential real estate market over the next generation, particularly within North Carolina, Idaho, Utah, California, Arizona, and New Jersey.

Trends in Labor Force and Electoral Power

Two other areas in which Latinos are an increasing presence and influence are the labor force and the ballot box. According to an analysis of U.S. Census Bureau data conducted by the Pew Hispanic Center, 23 million Latinos constituted 15 percent of the U.S. workforce in 2012, while 23.7 million Latinos stood eligible to vote in the 2012 presidential election (Taylor et al. 2012). According to a study undertaken by NERA Economic Consulting (Eisenach 2016), Latinos' increasing place in the U.S. labor force is attributable to (1) a higher rate of population increase among Latinos relative to the overall population; and (2) a higher rate of labor force participation among Latinos versus that of the general population, a rate of participation largely attributable to the younger age of the Latino population.

Latinos play a critical role in the U.S. labor force, not only as employees, but increasingly as entrepreneurs and job creators. According to the U.S. Department of Labor, Latino employment accounted for more than half of total U.S. job growth between 2000 and 2011, and expectations are that Latinos will continue to drive the growth of the nation's labor force over the next forty years (Acosta 2013; Bureau of Labor Statistics 2012). In addition, as of 2011 the rate of Latino participation in the labor force (65.9 percent) was higher than that of the general population (63.6 percent). Further, the unemployment rate of the Latino population has retreated from a peak of 13 percent in 2009 to 9.6 percent in 2011 (Bureau of Labor Statistics 2012). Non-Latino participation in the labor force over the next ten years will be affected by retirements among the "baby boomer" generation, leading to overall slower growth of the U.S. labor force relative to previous decades. The opposite, however, is true of the Latino population, whose participation will be augmented through both immigration and through large numbers of young people reaching employable age (Humphreys 2013). On the negative side with respect to economic potential, the Latino portion of the workforce is less likely be college educated than whites or African Americans. Approximately one in six employed Latinos aged twenty-five and over has completed a bachelor's degree, less than half the proportion among employed whites. This statistic can be somewhat correlated to the fact that Latinos are far more likely to be foreign born (education levels tend to be lower for immigrants than for native-born Americans). In 2011, 52.2 percent of the Latino labor force was foreign born compared to only 15.9 percent of the overall labor force (Bureau of Labor Statistics 2012). Regardless, Latinos are earning more. Forty percent of Latino households earned over $50,000 in 2011, and Latino households earning more than this figure are growing at a faster rate than in the general population (Acosta 2013).

With respect to entrepreneurship within the U.S. economy, Latinos are at the forefront. There is a growing consensus among modern economists that entrepreneurship and new business formation now account for a disproportionate share of job creation and economic growth. Research conducted by John Haltiwanger in 2012 suggests that the dynamic creation of new businesses is necessary to sustain job creation, productivity improvements, and overall growth in today's global economy. In recent years, the contributions of Latinos to this dynamism, as reflected in new business formation and entrepreneurships, have been disproportionate to their numbers. According to the U.S. Census Bureau Survey of Business

Owners, the number of Latino-owned firms more than doubled from 1.6 million to 3.3 million during the decade between 2002 and 2012.

Since the turn of the century Latino voters have steadily increased their political power, influencing political contests at all levels, including that of the presidency. The increased political influence has been accompanied by increased voter registration, which rose 54 percent between 2004 and 2008, while the rate of voter turnout climbed to 64 percent. According to the U.S Census Bureau, the Latino percentage of the total electorate increased from 7 percent in 2010 to 8.4 percent in 2012, a year in which a record number of Latinos cast ballots for a U.S. president. A Pew Hispanic Center analysis based on U.S. Census Bureau data (2012) found that whereas the nation's 53 million Latinos composed 17 percent of the total U.S. population, they constituted less than 10 percent of all voters in 2012. Latinos' total voting power is therefore not reflected by the actual number of people who cast their votes in in 2012 (Taylor et al. 2012). The same research suggests that the Latino electorate will rise quickly—perhaps doubling within a generation—for several reasons. The most important is that Latinos are by far the nation's youngest ethnic group. Their median age is twenty-seven years—and just eighteen years among native-born Latinos—compared with forty-two years for that of white non-Latinos (Taylor et al. 2012). In the coming decades, the Latino percentage of the age-eligible electorate will rise markedly through generational replacement alone. Projections by the Pew Hispanic Center estimate that Latinos will account for 40 percent of the growth in the eligible electorate in the United States between now and 2030, at which time 40 million Latinos will be eligible to vote, up from 23.7 million now.

The Latino vote is not only growing, but having a wider impact geographically. It is perhaps not surprising that Latino voters are making a significant political impact in major cities and the traditional gateway states of the Southwest and Florida, which have long-standing Latino communities. For instance, Texas and Florida saw voter turnout increase, respectively, by 31 percent and 81 percent between the 2000 and 2008 presidential elections. More surprising, however, are statistics related to "new immigrant" states. For example, Latino voter turnout between the 2000 and 2008 elections increased by 157 percent in South Carolina, 164 percent in Nevada, 250 percent in North Carolina, and 392 percent in Georgia (America's Voice 2010).

In terms of the 2016 potential and actual Latino electorate, findings of the Pew Hispanic Center note the following:

- Millennials constitute 44 percent of Latino eligible voters and are the fastest-growing segment of this electorate.
- Among millennial voters, 36 percent said they would be casting a ballot for the first time versus only 9 percent for non-millennial voters (ages thirty-six and older).
- Between 2012 and 2016, 3.2 million U.S.-born Latinos reached eighteen years of age, accounting for 80 percent of the increase in Latinos eligible to vote during this period.
- Latinos historically have viewed the Democratic Party as being more sensitive to Latino voters than the Republican Party, though the degree of this perception has fluctuated, depending on elections and candidates.
- The share of Latino registered voters dissatisfied with the nation's direction rose from 50 percent in 2012 to 57 percent in 2016.
- One in five Latino registered voters who planned to vote in 2016 were first-time voters.

When it comes to party affiliation, a 2016 Pew Research Center survey indicated that almost two-thirds (64 percent) of registered Latino voters either identified with or leaned toward the Democratic Party, with only 24 percent showing similar sentiments toward the Republican Party. However, these affiliations differ markedly among different Latino voting blocs. For example, approximately half of all Cuban American voters in Florida supported Donald Trump's candidacy in 2016. Cuban Americans constitute the third-largest group of Latinos within the United States, accounting for 3.7 percent of the U.S. Latino population in 2013 (Lopez 2015). In Florida, where two-thirds (67 percent) of the nation's 1.2 million Cuban Americans reside, Cuban Americans were approximately twice as likely as non-Cuban Latinos to cast ballots for Donald Trump. More than half (54 percent) supported the Republican president-elect compared with about a quarter (26 percent) of non-Cuban Latinos, according to national election exit poll data (Krogstad and Flores 2016).

Each year 800,000 Latinos turn eighteen, an annual statistic that could grow to one million by 2030, resulting in a potential sixteen million additional Latino voters by that year. This number would further swell should Congress pass a comprehensive immigration reform bill leading to citizenship for the more than seven million unauthorized Latino immigrants already living in the United States (Taylor et al. 2012). Many analysts have noted that as the Latino electorate grows in size and power, candidates from all political parties will have to become more cognizant of this electorate's views and opinions, or risk defeat in congressional and presidential races.

The Latino presence in the labor force and Latinos' electoral power has grown exponentially since 2000, resulting in a changing political landscape. Latino voters were pivotal to the victories of both President Barack Obama and congressional Democrats during the elections of 2008 and 2012. Therefore, candidates who want to count on the Latino vote need to do more than say a few words in Spanish. They need to support policies that recognize the contributions of Latinos and welcome immigrant Latinos into the American family.

Conclusion

The Latino population of the United States is growing fast and changing quickly. The places Latinos live, the jobs they hold, the schooling they complete, the languages they speak, and even their attitudes on key political and social issues are all in flux. Latinos already account for an important share of consumer expenditures, and given their youth, educational advances, and increasing buying power are rapidly becoming preeminent drivers of economic growth as well as likely trendsetters in the marketplace. It is imperative for marketers to understand the what, where, how, and why of their role in tomorrow's consumption sphere. As demographic and economic forces converge, Latinos will inspire and drive market trends. Currently, Latinos are leading the nation's postrecession housing recovery, a factor considered by many top economists to be the key to U.S. economic prosperity over the next thirty years (Acosta 2013). The evidence presented about the distinctiveness and sustainability of Latino influence in four key areas—demographics, market power, buying power, and labor force/electoral power—implies a future American culture with a strong Latino flavor.

Chapter 2

THE POWER OF PLACE AND NEIGHBORHOOD SELECTION

This chapter has three objectives. The first is to review some of the current literature on the concept of "placemaking" with respect to culture, a key element in Latino urbanism. The second is to identify principal areas of focus with respect to Latino urbanism, identifying consistencies as well as deficiencies in current literature. The third is to examine the two principal characteristics of "placemaking" as it affects the evolution of Latino neighborhoods in the United States, specifically: (1) the impact of culture on urban composition and neighborhood structure in the reappropriation process; and (2) the contribution of any sociocultural infrastructure and support networks afforded residents. Understanding these factors is crucial in forming explanations of why and how Latino neighborhoods develop in large urban areas and whether or not they continue to thrive.

Placemaking and Culture

Understanding the significance and value of the cultural landscape is crucial in the process of placemaking. Traditionally, planners, designers, and policy makers have attempted to impose their visions of acceptable use of space with a top-down process involving zoning codes and design regulations, while the actions of everyday users create adaptive but significant meaning of place in a bottom-up process, a process that is ignored or marginalized in most of our current urban planning and design methodologies. It is through the bottom-up process that people make attachments to places that are critical to maintaining well-being and/or minimizing distress (Hayden 1995). This is particularly the case with many immigrant neighborhoods in urban areas across the United States. Scholars have argued that an individual's sense of place is both a biological response to the surrounding physical environment and a cultural creation (Tuan 1977).

In other words, individuals familiarize themselves with a given place by engaging all their senses (sight, smell, hearing, touch, and taste).

Placemaking involves more than physical manipulations of space. Places can be both real and imagined; they depend on mental association as well as physical shape and character. Environmental psychologists Setha Low and Irvin Altman define this as "place attachment," one in which social relations between individuals are highly entwined with spatial perception. The psychological process of becoming attached to a place evolves in a manner similar to an infant's attachment to his or her parents. Slowly and subtly, places develop into sources of emotional strength (Altman and Low 1992). Place attachment develops as physical alterations are made to the public realm and memories are created within the public spaces. For instance, as the character of front yards and vacant lots changes, community murals and store frontages are painted, street amenities are added, and sidewalks and public parks become arenas of economic exchange, places of great significance emerge in urban spaces that might once have been dismissed as "banal" (Chase, Crawford, and Kaliski 1999, 2009; Lara 2012a,b; Oberle 2004, 2006; Rojas 1991).

Today, the term "placemaking" is used in many settings—not just by citizens and organizations committed to grassroots community improvement, but also by planners, community leaders, and developers who use it to establish a "brand" to imply authenticity and quality, even if their projects do not always live up to that promise (Project for Public Spaces 2017). Placemaking can be defined as the transformation process of physical space into areas that support human interaction, economic exchange, and well-being. The placemaking process is becoming recognized for its ability to enable collaborative frameworks and for its power to shift the behavior of citizens from that of passive consumers of services to actors, co-creators, and agents of change. Placemaking is a process initiated by groups of individuals and involves everything that can be observed at the eye level where what began as a mere street layout evolves into a series of networks of human interactions and activities—i.e., "places." This starts with citizens working together to improve their local environment. Placemaking is committed to "strengthening the connection between people and the places they share. Initiating this process makes little sense without the support of the affected community" (Glaser 2012).

Successful placemaking practices pay close attention to ways in which the physical, social, ecological, cultural, and even spiritual qualities of a place are intimately entwined.

Different methods and tools have been used to quantify and document the unique qualities and characteristics of place. For example, "cultural mapping" has recently become a popular technique among policy formulators. Essentially, this is a methodology undertaken to audit whatever aspect of local culture is being examined (creative industries, local community networks, relevant arts and community organizations, and so on) (Gibson 2010). Cultural mapping can help to develop a profile of how communities operate in places and to explain the functional links between commercial, artistic, and cultural expression. Cultural auditing, therefore, is a documentation of physical space.

During the 1960s and 1970s, Kevin Lynch used cognitive mapping as a tool for uncovering more comprehensive territorial information with respect to contemporary populations (Hayden 1995). Lynch studied mental/cognitive images of a given city by asking people to draw maps or give directions. Some of Lynch's findings revealed that residents of affluent white neighborhoods and those of inner-city African American neighborhoods and downtown immigrant working-class enclaves each had entirely different perceptions of spaces in the city (Lynch 1960). Each of the studied groups understood the city in terms of both its overall size and with respect to memorable features and landmarks. The cognitive maps demonstrated to urban planners, architects, and policy makers the need, on the one hand, to recognize how different ethnic and socioeconomic groups perceive and understand their city, and, on the other hand, to make the overall concept of the city more coherent and communicable to all residents.

Another simple way to document and quantify the qualities of space is through observation. Through observation we are capable of understanding what is going on around us. Some planners, architects, and landscape architects have been trained to observe and understand the on-the-ground context in order to assist in urban planning and to design place-specific solutions. Walking is a very powerful tool for observing and gaining knowledge of a city and its surroundings while immersing oneself in local culture. More than any other mode of transportation, walking allows the observer to control the pace of observation, experiencing far fewer distractions than he or she would in driving or even riding a bicycle (Jacobs 1993). Further, it may be the only means of reaching otherwise inaccessible places. Some of the tools used to document such an observation process are sketching, photographs, and informal interviews with local residents. According to Allan Jacobs (1993), the value of sketching is that it forces the observer to pay more attention to small details that would otherwise escape their notice. It is often in the noticing of small details that valuable clues are uncovered. For instance, the condition and maintenance of buildings might be evidence that changes are taking place in a given neighborhood. Effective observation can enable planners to make timely responses to challenges and opportunities in cities and neighborhoods.

One of the most important but least researched aspects of urban space is the impact of culture and ethnicity on placemaking and the consequent adaptation of the physical space in question. Lack of serious attention to this cultural aspect has too often characterized the work of urban planners and policy makers. The contribution that specific cultures make to urban resiliency—particularly in older and/or neglected neighborhoods suffering from lack of capital investment—is only partially recognized, when it is not ignored altogether.

Unfortunately, a lack of interest in cultural factors has characterized the "suburban" model of planning that has dominated urban planning in American cities over the past half century. Consequent planning and design strategies have tended to limit life experiences beyond home and work, resulting in "dormitory zones" deficient in communal space and where cars represent virtually the sole means of mobility. Real-world experience is substituted with electronic imagery, and the "social realm becomes less and less real" (Banerjee 2001; Mitchell 1996; Touraine 1988) Through a pervasive separation of uses and services, planners and designers have failed to provide places where people can interact and celebrate cultural differences, such as the local pub or coffee house (Oldenburg 2001).

It is in older and neglected inner-city and suburban neighborhoods that the role of culture within immigrant communities is essential to economic revitalization and placemaking. Several important researchers argue that immigrant populations are key to the recovery, reinvention, and economic revitalization of American downtowns, inner-city neighborhoods, and older suburbs (Agius 2012; Aronson 1997; Bernstein 2005; Fishman 2005; Logan 2003; Myers 1999). While on the one hand the revitalization of urban neighborhoods by immigrants is celebrated, on the other hand, there are cases in which neighborhoods that are gentrified can become a "victim of their own success." It is important to acknowledge the vulnerabilities of ethnic neighborhoods to the increasing popularity of urban life among artists and the highly educated. For the past twenty years many inner cities have begun to thrive again through gentrification, but the movement of the wealthy and upwardly mobile to these areas has placed intense pressure on rents and real estate prices, aggravating the economic straits of local businesses and low-income ethnic communities. These impacts are particularly pronounced in what were once the traditionally Latino urban districts of Los Angeles, New York, San Francisco, and Chicago (Hwang and Sampson 2014; Romero Gonzalez and Lejano 2009; Sampson 2012). Noteworthy examples of this side effect of gentrification include the Mission District of San Francisco, Lincoln Heights and Highland Park in Los Angeles, East Harlem in New York, and Pilsen and Humboldt Park in Chicago. Policies and strategies that address this issue are critically needed, and some recommendations will be provided in later chapters.

Overview of Current Literature on Latino Urbanism

For the past few years Latinos have been impacting the built environment and public realm in dynamic ways that are more conducive to cultural (re)adaptations while contributing to the social and economic development of urban and suburban neighborhoods and commercial corridors. Latinos contribute to the urban revitalization process by (re)appropriating space for their own use, turning downtrodden areas into vibrant commercial and residential centers to suit the needs and cultural preferences of transnational immigrants. This movement is known as Latino urbanism, an emerging approach to planning, design, and development that responds to Latino lifestyles, cultural preferences, and economic needs that are reflected in the built environment. Latino urbanism is reflected in the way Latinos bring key qualities that are essential to the revitalization process of our cities, including socialization, leisure activities, and commerce. It is a design and planning concept based on how Latinos organize and use space. Proponents of this movement argue that Latino urban living in modern American towns and cities can incorporate many of the principal tenets of new urbanism and sustainable urbanism: compact urban form, pedestrian activity, public transportation, sustainability, recycling, and active use of public and private spaces. Latino urbanism strategies show designers, public policy makers, academics, and business owners examples of enabling approaches in which Latino communities can revitalize suburban neighborhoods and obsolete and underutilized retail corridors, improving both the local economy and the quality of life for residents.

Scholars have focused on the implications of the growing Latino population in this country and its impacts on the dynamics of our built environment. The relevant literature highlights the increasing presence of Latinos and their role in shaping and incorporating cultural needs in the development of American metropolises (Davis 2001; Delgado 2011; Diaz 2005; Diaz and Torres 2012; New America Alliance Institute 2014). Key areas of study include emerging new geographies and the sociopolitical constructions in cities and regions (Malavé and Giordani 2015; Odem and Lacy 2009; Valle and Torres 2000). Specific topics that define Latino urbanism include the appropriation and readaptation of physical space for new purposes based on cultural expression and the emergence of multiethnic coalitions. In the last fifteen years a number of edited books and special issues of journals have provided comprehensive approaches to the study of Latino spaces (Arreola 2005; Diaz and Torres 2012; Gonzalez 2017; Lara 2012a,b; Rios, Vazquez, and Miranda 2012).

Throughout the literature review specific topics and key focus areas emerged that provide a broader geographical and thematic discussion of the conflicts, challenges, and changes in different settings and locations. Each one of these key areas tackles specific aspects of placemaking practices in Latino urbanism, and sometimes case studies are used to illustrate major points. Six key areas of focus emerged from this literature review, including (1) Latino places and urban places, (2) everyday Latino urbanism, (3) reclaimed/readapted spaces, (4) contested space, (5) uncovering the economic reinterpretation of place, and (6) participatory and inclusionary approaches.

LATINO PLACES AND URBAN SPACES

In this focus area authors examine how Latino communities are at the center of many place-based struggles, given the heightened attention to immigration and citizenship issues. Discussion of these struggles provides a means to analyze, interrogate, and reflect on contemporary meaning and perception of place and cultural readaptations among Latino communities. Some of the authors trace the history of Latinos' struggle for adequate housing opportunities from the nineteenth century to the recent national mortgage crisis and today's anti-immigration policies and sentiments. Authors also analyze the legal hurdles that prevent better housing opportunities, as well as how declining industrial employment and massive urban renewal projects have carved out distinct geographical and racial places (Diaz and Torres 2012; New America Alliance Institute 2014; Herzog 2006; Irazábal 2009; Irazábal and Farhat 2012; Valle and Torres 2000). Some authors have also examined the implications of transborder Latin American sociocultural and spatial conditions across the globe and at different scales, from gendered and racialized individuals to national and transnational organizations (Herzog 2006; Irazábal 2014; Irazábal and Farhat 2012). The development policies that pressure Latinos to assimilate to the established U.S. notions of appropriate space use and how they undercut the economic, social, and environmental benefits inherent in the Latino lifestyle are assessed as well (Diaz 2005; Diaz and Torres 2012; Mendez 2005).

EVERYDAY LATINO URBANISM

This study area focuses on topics related to the appropriation of space and the implications of everyday urbanism and space dynamics (Arreola 2012; Chase, Crawford, and Kaliski 1999, 2009; Kim 2012; Rios, Vazquez, and Miranda 2012; Rojas 1991). It deals with the manner in which both public and private spaces can be temporarily or permanently transformed based on cultural needs. It details how Latinos claim space as they struggle to build community and gain social and political stability in the urban context. Examples of how different Latino immigrant groups transform and modify everyday urban space are provided and the cultural impact on the built environment assessed. Also examined are placemaking practices of working-class and impoverished Latinos from the ground up (Angotti 2012; Chase, Crawford, and Kaliski 1999, 2009; Lara 2012b; Londoño 2010; Rios, Vazquez, and Miranda 2012; Rojas 1991; Vergara et al. 1999). The overall focus is on how public spaces are claimed by Latino immigrants and how they bring their own and different uses of urban space to an already built environment. Topics covered include mobility, home life, religious life, and the prevalence and use of recreational and open space.

RECLAIMED/READAPTED SPACES

This study area is centered on the adaptive reuse of spaces and the social, economic, and cultural ramifications that such practices have on community revitalization processes (Arreola 2012; Gonzalez 2017; Irazábal 2009). Also examined is the impact of adaptive reuse of abandoned, obsolete, or dilapidated areas for new collective purposes or cultural representation. Highlighted is how Latinos create place through use, inhabitation, and building practices and the challenges and opportunities this presents to professional placemakers, such as urban designers, planners, policy makers, architects, and landscape architects. Case studies in both small towns and urban areas describe instances where immigrant communities have transformed residential landscapes and altered existing community space to reflect Latino culture (Arreola 2012; Dieterlen 2015; Lara 2012a,b; Latorre 2009). A principal point of cultural identification in such cases for immigrants has often been religion (Irazábal and Gómez-Barris 2007).

CONTESTED SPACE

This area of study involves attaching a new interpretation and meaning to Latino spaces in diverse locations. It also analyzes the forces that shape those places, providing critical perspectives on the role of planning and development (Flippen and Parrado 2012; Irazábal and Gómez-Barris 2007; Rios, Vazquez, and Miranda 2012). Examined are the conflicts and struggles related to the identity of place. Attention is drawn to the role of collective action in placemaking and to the efforts of planning and design professionals in identifying the elements that contribute to the development of place in our cities. Cases where tensions between Latino immigrants and municipal governments have existed are addressed, as is the overall failure on the part of authorities to recognize the contributions Latinos have made to urban planning and development, both academically and commercially (Carpio,

Irazábal, and Pulido 2011; Diaz and Torres 2012; Lejano and González 2017; Onésimo and Jennings 2012; Sandoval and Maldonado 2010). Authors explore the implications of placemaking in the transformation of homogeneous non-Latino white communities toward new dynamic, multicultural places (Agius 2012; Diaz and Torres 2012; Sandoval and Maldonado 2012).

UNCOVERING THE ECONOMIC REINTERPRETATION OF PLACE

This study area relates to "the multifarious ways in which ethnic groups intersect with almost any sort of economic activity" (Kaplan and Li 2006, 2–3). It examines how ethnic entrepreneurs, employees, and customers can earn a living and/or obtain familiar specialty products while at the same time contributing positively to the local economy. Tensions and struggles related to identity of place are explored, as is a reinterpretation of hidden meaning with respect to place (Diaz and Torres 2012; Irazábal 2009; Sandoval and Maldonado 2012). A key aspect of the reinterpretation of place involves a focus on the economic contribution of Latino small businesses. These entrepreneurial ventures provide social, economic, and cultural comfort to their communities. They serve as excellent facilitators of community capacity, a key feature of effective social work practice. Some scholars have extensively explored the multifaceted roles that small businesses play in Latino communities and their potential for improving social as well as well as economic conditions there (Delgado 1997, 2007, 2011). Case studies involving empirical research and discussions with respect to Latino urbanism demonstrate the manner in which Latinxs are shaping the cultural, social, economic, and physical geographies of communities throughout the United States. Of particular importance are the rediscovery of public space and the role of culture and commerce in its reinterpretation. Further emphasized is how political economy, migration, and cultural differences affect and provide a context for planning, decisions, and methods of policy implementation (Delgado 1997; Flippen and Parrado 2012; Irazábal and Gómez-Barris 2007; Rios 2009).

PARTICIPATORY AND INCLUSIONARY APPROACHES

This area of study and research relates to the relationship between place and cultural identity, drawing on examples from both rural and urban settings to illustrate how Latino communities engage in place-making processes through inclusive forms of empowerment and civic engagement. Through such engagement, immigrant Latino communities gain voice and develop their capacity to participate in the public realm through a bottom-up process (Emerson 2012; González et al. 2012; Trabalzi and Sandoval 2010; Zapata 2012). Scholars note that successful community engagement and citizen empowerment can be characterized by such pluralistic practices as formal public meetings, charettes, public involvement workshops, and online websites encouraging comments (González 2017; González et al. 2012; Kim 2012; Lara 2012b; Zapata 2012). They further note that effective organization and research can provide a more comprehensive view of underlying issues regarding urban development, and that any successful urban planning for multicultural communities must encourage the participation of such communities in a spirit that embraces both diversity and a sense of justice (Kotin, Dyrness, and Irazábal 2011; Trabalzi and Sandoval 2010; Zapata 2012).

While far from exhaustive, the literature review above summarizes the manner in which Latino urbanism and placemaking have evolved theoretically and how the prevailing rhetoric of place, identity, and authenticity are now commonly understood as points of reference for everyday practice. The review of relevant literature concerning Latino urbanism further reveals several dimensions of placemaking that address image (re)construction through historical, social, political, and economic issues. The review also reveals gaps between the implications of Latino urbanism for the character and physical design of space and its potential for sustainability in the urban environment. These gaps are addressed in the following chapter.

Effects of Placemaking in Latino Neighborhoods

This section examines the two fundamental characteristics of "placemaking" as it affects the evolution of Latino communities in the United States, specifically: (1) the impact of culture on urban composition and neighborhood structure in the reappropriation process; and (2) the contribution of any sociocultural infrastructure or support networks afforded residents.

CULTURAL IMPLICATIONS IN URBAN COMPOSITION AND NEIGHBORHOOD STRUCTURE

The cultural dimension of a given neighborhood can no longer be ignored during the planning and design process (Hall 1990, 42). Some prominent urban scholars argue that the idea of creating a community through deterministic designs must be reevaluated as well. They suggest that consideration of patterns of class, culture, race, and ethnicity should be an integral part of the redevelopment process for urban communities (Harvey 1997, 1; Marcuse 2000, 4). Although planning models for design, development, and revitalization such as New Urbanism have proven value in building scale and form, they too often fail to consider cultural factors. Current planning models that focus on the use and accommodation of the automobile have the effect of fragmenting an individual's cultural network and contributing to social alienation. Further, they have exacerbated environmental problems such as air pollution and traffic congestion. Planners and policy makers have also largely failed to accept their responsibility in contributing to critical irrationalities in land-use policy and practice (Diaz and Torres 2012).

Cities evolve and adapt continuously, and though the essence of local culture, people, and place is so important in this adaptation, it is routinely ignored when master plans or design guidelines are adopted and implemented. Everyday urban activities can help to mitigate the impacts of urban change. In many cities across the United States, Latino entrepreneurs have succeeded in dynamically transforming the urban fabric and public infrastructure in ways that are more conducive to cultural adaptation. Socialization, leisure activities, and commerce have all been influenced by their efforts. These entrepreneurs have succeeded because of their recognition of the commanding role of the family in Latino culture. Latino families are central to the happiness and resilience of Latino communities everywhere. Daily activities such as gathering for a meal, playing and watching sports, taking walks, and enjoying the outdoors are examples of how Latinos actively engage in sustaining relationships with their friends and family. In Latino neighborhoods the need for spaces where these activities can take place has driven the adaptation or conversion of former offices and residential and historic buildings into ethnic food markets, bars, restaurants, bridal shops, beauty salons, and specialty stores where residents can interact and connect with others while simultaneously contributing to the social and economic revitalization of the area.

The contemporary American notion of public space has been greatly impacted by zoning regulations and land-use planning, both of which have often fragmented and undermined public places and public life in our cities. Under these conditions, pedestrian streets, squares, plazas, and promenades are becoming obsolete and/or unrecognizable. They are no longer the principal forums where people meet other people and socialize (Banerjee 2001, 9; Ellin 2006, 9). Some authors argue that the contemporary city has shifted from an era of decentralization to one of "despatialization" (Carmona and Tiesdell 2007, 3; Herzog 2006, 27; Mitchell 1996, 106). Most infrastructure since World War II has been designed to accommodate the automobile, leading to an urban sprawl in which traditional public spaces have lost much of their attractiveness. It has been argued that planners and designers no longer design places for communities with the local environment in mind (Beatley and Manning1997, 54; Ellin 2006, 12; Kunstler 1994, 22). Many of the new public spaces in contemporary America are indoor shopping malls, strip malls, freeways, TV screens, and rigorously planned and subsidized "historic districts" that are supported by local chambers of commerce (Banerjee 2001; Knox 1993, 68; Kunstler 1994, 175; Loukaitou-Sideris and Banerjee 1998, 175; Sorkin 1992, 206; Winnick 1990, 49). However, these definitions of public space are now shifting with the arrival of new waves of Latino immigrants. In urban centers the growing numbers and increased purchasing power of Latinos (as discussed in the previous chapter) have caused a shift in consumption patterns and demands for products and services. This set of conditions has triggered the revitalization of neglected urban neighborhoods whose physical characteristics present ideal conditions for the establishment of ethnic entrepreneurial businesses.

Traditionally the character of a city is defined by its streets and public spaces. Streets play a critical role in cities, connecting spaces, goods, and people, as well as facilitating commerce, social interaction, and mobility in the process of revitalization. Successful urban design always takes into account not only the physical characteristics of streets, public spaces, and buildings, but their individual functions and relationships to each other. Research has shown that well-connected street networks and properly designed buildings encourage not only improvements to the overall character of the neighborhood but also stimulate economic activities and enhance functionality (Banerjee 2001; Carmona and Tiesdell 2007; Kostof and Tobias 2003; Oldenburg 2001; Sucher 2003). This means taking into account an urban area's composition as well as its buildings in the design process. Where the physical environment along an urban or suburban ethnic corridor has been adapted to the respective community's "rules" with respect to retail trade, foot traffic, parking, and residential lifestyle, as well as to the relationships between these considerations, conditions are optimized for commercial development and/or neighborhood revitalization. These conditions are generally met in ethnic corridors of the early twenty-first century, or what Peter Calthorpe refers as areas of "transit-oriented development" (Calthorpe and Fulton 2001). In most cases residential areas close to city centers are already well served by surviving transit lines, with population densities that make them excellent candidates for the revival of trolley car networks. The scale of residential housing that remains in these areas is often well adapted to the smaller, nontraditional households as well. Most buildings are designed with the incorporation of retail establishments at their street level in mind. Such retail outlets often feature engaging window displays to capitalize on the heavy pedestrian traffic that characterizes a neighborhood less dependent on the automobile for mobility. All of these features of an optimally designed urban neighborhood are conducive to experiencing the city at the eye level, which is how most people relate to the city or the "public realm" (Carmona and Tiesdell 2007; Condon and Yaro 2010; Gehl 2011; Gehl and Svarre 2013; Jacobs 1993). The public realm includes façades of buildings, sidewalks, parking areas, street amenities, and other aspects of the built environment. Attention to elements at the eye level is part of any successful revitalization of retail and commercial activity, and this is why its consideration is so important in building design. The basic arrangement of the building on the site under consideration is far more important than what usually passes for architecture: the exterior appearance and "envelope" of the structure (Sucher 2003).

The amount of foot traffic generated by the "twenty-first-century corridors" has generally been enough to sustain a diverse array of retail establishments as well as to promote their expansion. This process has been driven by immigrants, risk-takers by nature who, unusually successful as entrepreneurs, are statistically twice as likely as native-born Americans to start their own firms (McDaniel 2014). Most of the buildings in the corridors have been adapted for traditional mixed use: shops and stores on the street level and living quarters on the floors above. Parking is generally permitted on the streets facing retail establishments. The corridors have attracted local and regional entrepreneurs and niche businesses geared to the Latino market: in particular, art-related businesses and organizations, ethnic supermarkets, restaurants, and routine services such as dry cleaning.

According to David Sucher (Sucher 2003, 40), buildings within any "twenty-first-century corridor" must meet "the three basic rules of retail":

1. *Buildings must be erected to the sidewalk to create a "streetwall."* Building to the sidewalk or property line creates a strong "streetwall" in which each building meets or comes close to the sidewalk to accommodate pedestrians. The sidewalk is important because it channels pedestrian movements and places people into closer proximity to one another, enhancing the opportunity for human contact and social interaction.

2. *The front of a building must be permeable.* The front of any building should be permeable in the sense that the building's interior is connected with sidewalks through windows and doors, rather than by blank walls, facilitating connections between individuals inside and outside of the building. It is also important that pedestrians be able to view the merchandise a store has on sale as well as its patrons.

3. *No parking lots in front of buildings.* It is essential to put on-site parking lots above, below, behind, or beside a building, so as not to obstruct pedestrian flow. On-street parking should be allowed, however, to accommodate retail patrons in a hurry.

Implementation of the "three basic rules of retail" facilitates a more pedestrian-friendly environment, and therefore a more social one, something often forgotten in current planning and development practices that are centered on automobile use. Crowded,

Figure 2. Example of a livable community and street structure that follows the urban design rules. The three qualities of urban design are present throughout the building stock in the neighborhood, facilitating adaptive use for commercial purposes. Image by author.

commercially lively areas composed almost entirely of pedestrians are part of Latino culture. Such areas are typical of all Latin America cities. Moreover, they are not the gathering points for merely commercial activity, but for much, if not most, of a day's social interaction.

The cultural diversity that Latinos are bringing to the United States is not merely altering sociocultural relations but transforming the physical landscape as well. Latino immigrants have turned lifeless, economically moribund suburban areas developed with only automobile transport in mind into lively, crowded areas filled with pedestrians enjoying traditionally urban activities. In discussing this transformation, many scholars have discussed the shifts in the meaning and identity of public space that have accompanied it (Chase, Crawford, and Kaliski 1991, 30; Diaz 2005, 263; Herzog 2006, 62; Kyvig and Marty 2000, 42; Winnick 1990, 9). Chase, Crawford, and Kaliski (1999) have noted that immigrants have redefined the concept of public space because of their cultural practices and life experience. Latino immigrants more often than not were raised in urban areas where cities were designed around such public spaces as town squares, plazas, gardens, and major commercial thoroughfares (Herzog 2006, 62). Such patterns in urban design can be traced to the period of Spanish colonial rule under the Laws of the Indies, a period of administration that spans almost three hundred years. The Laws of the Indies established standards for new settlement in Spain's colonies that are still very much in evidence in Latin America today (Kostof and Tobias 2003, 124). The consequence was that, unlike in North America, the pattern of settlement and urban development in Latin America was largely *planned*, guided by legislation and codes enacted by the Spanish Crown (Rodriguez 2005, 353–54). While there was some adaptation to individual geographical considerations, these settlement codes led to the remarkably homogeneous nature of urban centers under Spanish control, even if they were thousands of miles apart, as were Lima and Mexico City. Cities in Latin America would develop far more rapidly than in North America, as they were key elements in the colonization process as centers for the administration of political, military, and religious authority. Cities also were the centers of most commercial activity and almost all trade, trade being tightly regulated by Spain in its own interest of largely monopolizing it (Rodriguez 2005, 353–54). The idea of *place* is therefore as much a historical phenomenon as a cultural affinity of Latin Americans. Nor is it surprising that so many Latin American immigrants have brought to the United States the embrace of public life inspired by Spanish planning, in so doing transforming some of the most hostile urban and suburban environments of their new homeland. Once sterile environments composed of streetscapes and vacant lots alien to Latino culture are now lively zones of commercial and social activity characterized by an "open air" ambience where street vendors sell tacos, fruit, art, blankets, and religious souvenirs.

Studies demonstrate that immigrants strengthen urban economies and revitalize economically depressed neighborhoods. They are credited with helping to reverse the decay of inner cities while simultaneously augmenting the labor force, consumer demand, trade, and other economic stimuli (Aronson 1997, 5; Delgado 1997; Eroglu 2002, 55; Hayduk 1998). New immigrants have also revitalized working-class neighborhoods as well as largely abandoned strip malls and commercial buildings. Some examples of cultural and commercial districts that have benefited from such revitalization efforts are Bronzeville in Chicago, the Fillmore and Mission Districts in San Francisco, the Greenwood District in Tulsa, the Broadway District in Los Angeles, and Little Saigon in San Diego. The notion that these ethnic corridors are the new "Main Street" or business district of the surrounding residential areas has increased commercial and social activity along all these corridors. Many are now "twenty-four hour" venues, with entirely different activities taking place depending on time of day (or night).

Another consideration in understanding the cultural aspects of the physical form and structure of Latino neighborhoods is the "Latino look" of storefront presentations. Urban Latino neighborhood configurations generally are characterized by (a) rules of retail, foot traffic, parking, residential mixes, and connections to residential streets; (b) main-street-in-action programming, hours of use, and daily patterns; and (c) a Latino look to storefront presentation and signage as well as uniquely Latino smells and sounds that are critical to this process. Ordinary landscapes are an important archive of social experience and cultural meaning, as they can reveal changes taking place in local subcultures as well as shifts in national, dominant cultural values (Meinig, Wand, and Jackson 1979, 149). A closer look at the transformations taking place in the urban landscape reveals areas now rich in social and cultural activity. Latino immigrants have made a highly visible investment in neighborhoods' building stocks. Many of the buildings from the early to mid-1900s have recently been reappropriated with an attractive Latino look that includes colorful façades and catchy signage.

When immigrants come to the United States, they bring cultural traits that influence how they use public spaces and carry out social life. The new urban spaces they occupy often involve culturally specific uses and reflect culturally specific meanings, resulting in new forms of fixed and temporary public/private spaces and an increase in ethnic visibility. The emerging ethnic identity may be presented through public art, at bus stops, at garage sales, in street vending, in advertisements, in livery, on bulletin boards, and in the uses of vacant lots and adjacent streets. These forms of expression demonstrate some of the ways in which Latino urban residents are redefining conventional urban spaces. In ethnic commercial corridors, businesses use graffiti, flags, and murals of pastoral scenes from Latin American countries to inexpensively assert their identities and claim ownership of the area. The use of colors and graphics in advertisements for products and services provides strong visual statements that signal the presence of specific ethnic groups. National flags are often flown outside stores and shops. If customers are looking for specific products and goods that are common to Mexico, Guatemala, or El

Figure 3. Examples of Latino flavor include colors, textures, images, sounds, and smells. (1) Mexicantown, Detroit; (2) La Mega Michoacana Market, Columbus; (3) Grand Central Market, Los Angeles. Photos by author.

Salvador, the flags or other iconic elements peculiar to the individual country indicate where to look. Another important element in the décor is the use of religious symbols. Mexico's Virgin of Guadalupe is one such popular icon in many stores.

Food is an intrinsic part of Latin American culture. Its sharing is an important way in which family members and friends can relate to one other. It is available everywhere in ethnic corridors, whether from street vendors or mobile "taquerias" to the most exclusive and expensive of restaurants. Food, like the colors and icons, is a visual cue used by entrepreneurs to engage regular customers and to entice new ones.

The cultural factors that influence an urban area's complexion can provide clues to the phenomenon of "reappropriation." Latinos reappropriate abandoned and dilapidated buildings and structures such as gas stations, department stores, office buildings, single-family homes, and signs with the intention of using them for a new purpose. The result may be a bridal and special-occasion clothing shop, a convenience store, a restaurant, an auto-related services company, or any one of countless possibilities. Based on informal interviews with shop owners and residents, as well as on observations in the study areas between 2006 and 2013, there does not seem to be any prescribed pattern to the conversions undertaken. The nature of the adaptation appears to be merely a function of demand for services and the availability of building stock. Therefore, without any semblance of a master plan, Latinos have been gradually transforming the front yards, sidewalks, abandoned buildings, and vacant lots of blighted areas into vibrant economic zones with a strong sense of community (Chase, Crawford, and Kaliski 1999, 26; Ramati 1981). Such development is usually accompanied by sociocultural infrastructure support networks represented by churches, nonprofit organizations, schools, and employment centers.

What Latinos have accomplished is to develop a dynamic "open air" culture out of streetscapes, vacant lots, and derelict public facilities in areas that were not intended or designed to support either themselves or their culture. Examples of this practice include the appropriation of marginal and overlooked sites selected for their accessibility and convenience by street vendors selling tacos, fruit, art, blankets, or religious souvenirs, as well as the creation of temporary

Figure 4. Food is an essential component in the creation of more livable communities: (1) Bakery in Mexicantown, Detroit; (2) La Mega Michoacana Market, Columbus; (3) La Plaza Tapatia, Columbus. Photos by author.

day labor camps on unused land across from home improvement stores like Home Depot or Lowe's.

The transformation of derelict strip malls into Latino cultural hubs is particularly noticeable on weekends, when residents flock there to do their weekly shopping. Entire districts are filled with the sounds and smells emanating from the stores and restaurants lining the streets. These activities give these ethnic corridors a distinct character, one that reflects the clientele. The businesses further contribute to an active street life, with children, young adults, and the elderly all engaged in social interactions as shops are visited and transactions made. The areas therefore promote social cohesion and some measure of psychological support to members of the community.

The indicators of the success of a corridor include the presence of successful businesses, of establishments providing neighborhood residents and visitors with goods and services at reasonable prices, as well as the creation of a culture of opportunity and success.

THE PRESENCE OF SOCIAL INFRASTRUCTURE AND SUPPORT NETWORKS

The presence of locally based social capital is critical for the development of socially sustainable communities and the creation of social cohesion in immigrant neighborhoods. In the case of Latino corridors, the presence of social networks has an impact on (1) cultural adaptation, (2) job search outcomes, and (3) economic advancement. Social networks involve social interactions among participants with the aim of fostering a sense of belonging within a more or less defined social grouping (Chavis and Wandersman 1990). Social capital has been described as the intangible resources that exist in relationships between individuals (Coleman 1998). It also refers to the trust-based relationships that give those who have access to them an advantage compared to those who do not (Ong and Loukaitou-Sideris 2006). Social capital emphasizes how social networks can help prevent feelings of isolation and marginalization among immigrants and new residents. Social networks are the product of social capital and are crucial for advancement and participation in a new culture or environment.

For recent immigrants, ethnic businesses represent part of a social network that is also a link to their home countries: the

Figure 5. The new Latino commercial corridors are contributing to the local economic revitalization of cities and neighborhoods. Examples of this include (1) adaptive use of abandoned and obsolete suburban shopping malls, Columbus, Ohio; (2) upkeep and maintenance of residential areas, Mexicantown, Detroit; and (3) the rebirth of the corridor as the main street, southwest Detroit. Photos by author.

businesses provide a way to keep in close contact with the culture and way of life they left behind. In most cases, businesses are named after establishments or locales in the owner's home country (Oberle 2006).

The assimilation and adaptation process of newcomers to a neighborhood and/or urban environment depends on accessibility to existing social networks and "third places." The benefits of social networks are many, but most importantly they provide opportunities for social interaction among the participants as well as a sense of belonging. The most basic social network for Latino immigrants is the family. Other types of social networks include those formed on the basis of shared territory in a native country or on shared places of birth and life experiences, as well as those based on cultural characteristics, religion, or advocacy. Members of these networks often have similar aspirations and concerns about the quality of life in their communities. Briggs de Souza (1998) highlights two different types of networks: the ones that help people just to "get by" and those that help people to "get ahead." The main difference between these two types of networks is that those of the "get by" variety tend to offer emotional and personal support such as companionship, services like childcare, and small loans of food or tools; they further help in emergency situations. For recent immigrants, these types of networks are very valuable because they help them navigate under new sociocultural circumstances. They are usually provided by relatives, friends, and neighbors. The purpose of the "get ahead" networks is to link individuals to the outside world by offering access to resources and opportunities for more permanent advancement. These are the types of networks that help people change their quality of life through an improved economic outlook.

Research by Ong and Loukaitou-Sideris identified three major beneficial functions of social networks: (1) they act as buffers that protect individuals from stress (e.g., the establishment of familiar places where language, food, and/or sports are common to all members alleviates stress associated with homesickness); (2) they provide instrumental social support that allows new immigrants to assimilate faster; and (3) they act as sources of employment information and referrals (Ong and Loukaitou-Sideris 2006). In particular, survival and advancement in a new country depends on effective connections to social networks that foster economic development and provide links to job opportunities. Social networks like these are especially important for recent immigrants, who are often unaware of how the labor market functions in the United States (Eroglu 2002; Ong and Loukaitou-Sideris 2006; Thorp 2004; Winnick 1990).

The assimilation and adaptation process of new immigrants to their neighborhoods and urban environments depends on the accessibility of existing social networks. The benefits of social networks are many, but most importantly they provide both opportunities for social interaction among the participants and a sense of belonging. In addition to the sociocultural support networks, the establishment of ethnic commercial businesses and services contributes to a sense of pride in an area and plays an important role in the social structure of immigrant communities (Aronson 1997, 4; Delgado 1997; Eroglu 2002, 59; Ong and Loukaitou-Sideris 2006, 145; Thorp 2004). Latino small businesses play an influential role in a community that goes beyond the commercial establishment (Delgado 1997, 445–53). According to Levitt (1995), Latino owners of commercial establishments are motivated by more than money: they are also motivated by a sense of "social responsibility" that translates into providing culturally appropriate help for customers in need. Latino businesses can take on the role of nontraditional social networks by providing financial assistance, counseling, or advice, as well as by furnishing further information on formal and informal resources for assistance (Delgado 1997).

One of the most important aspects of the immigrant relationship to space is that immigrants are contributing to the creation of what Ray Oldenburg refers to as "third places"—the other two places being home and work—or "great good places," which are neutral public places where people gather to celebrate a common culture (Oldenburg 2001). According to Oldenburg, a third place is a generic designation for a great variety of public spaces that host regular, voluntary, informal, and happily anticipated gatherings of individuals beyond the realms of home and work. Examples of third places include cafés, bars, and public squares and plazas. The first place is the home, which is important and predictable for a growing child and will help to shape the individual's development through life. The second place is where we work, where the sole focus is on the productivity of the individual. Workplaces are also meant to instill competition among individuals and motivate people to advance professionally, while at the same time providing a source of income or compensation for the work or services provided. Third places are an important part of our daily life because they help us to relax and unwind from the stresses of home and work. In some cultures third places are an important part of daily life and constitute a priority. In Mediterranean and Latin American countries, the core of public life is located in third places, while in the United States third places rank very low and are not believed to have any real importance (Oldenburg 2001). Authors such as Banerjee (2001), Herzog (2006), Jacobs (2001), Loukaitou-Sideris and Banerjee (1998), and Shaftoe (2008) have written that such places are becoming extinct in contemporary American culture because private homes and the Internet have supplanted them as the principal forums in which to socialize and entertain. Latino immigrants, as we see in studies on Latino New Urbanism (González and Lejano 2009; Mendez 2005; Rojas 1991), place value on plazas, boulevards, gardens, and other physical elements that contribute to the creation of vibrant public places. When these elements are not present in the urban fabric, though, Latinos adapt to local conditions. Nontraditional settings, such as ethnic markets, food trucks, convenience stores, or butcher shops, become "third places" where individuals can gather to purchase a product or a service as well as to congregate for social purposes (Delgado 1997, 2007). Latinos conceive of and relate to urban life in their own social and cultural ways. It is through their "third places" that Latinos can facilitate conversations, exchange concerns, and advise or relate to their fellow citizens, becoming active participants in the daily life of their cities.

Ordinary landscapes are an important archive of social experience and cultural meaning, as they can reveal changes taking place in local subcultures as well as shifts in cultural values (Meinig, Wand, and Jackson 1979). In the case of ethnic corridors, a closer look at the transformations taking place in the urban landscape reveals areas now rich in social and cultural activity. The investment Latino immigrants have made in their neighborhoods is highly visible in their building stocks, many of which have been recently renovated with attractive and colorful façades.

Figure 6. The new Latino corridors offer diverse types of businesses and services that contribute to the creation of destination centers. Some of these places are well known for their Latino cuisine, specialty foods and products, and clothing stores for special occasions: (1) Mexicantown, southwest Detroit; (2) Morse Road Corridor, Columbus; and (3) West Vernor–Bagley Street Corridor, southwest Detroit. Photos by author.

Conclusion

The establishment of ethnic commercial businesses and services contributes to economic revitalization and a sense of pride in ethnic neighborhoods. Ethnic businesses also play an important role in the social structure of immigrant communities, as do the multiple informal associations in which Latino immigrants engage that revolve around social-tie networks, such as family, school, and church. Research by authors and scholars supports the idea that strong social networks and social capital are integral to the economic development and social sustainability of individuals and communities, especially for new immigrants (Aronson 1997; Delgado 1997; Eroglu 2002; Ong 2006; Thorp 2004). From an economic perspective, inner-city commercial revitalizations have an impact in three distinct and overlapping areas of which immigrants are an integral part: (1) neighborhood revitalization, (2) retail development, and (3) minority entrepreneurship (Sutton 2010). Critical attention to the impact of culture on urban composition and to the presence of social infrastructure and support networks suggests strategies for promoting and enhancing cultural and economic resilience in ethnic neighborhoods.

UNVEILING LATINO URBANISM CASE STUDIES

Introduction

The economic contribution of immigrants in highly skilled fields of occupation is generally well known, but the role that blue-collar immigrants play in revitalizing economically depressed communities, through both manual labor and small-business entrepreneurship, is either less frequently addressed or ignored altogether. Numerous studies have documented that immigration has reemerged over the past twenty-five years as a powerful force, influencing the size and complexion of the population in U.S. urban centers. According to economist David Card (2007), immigrants' impact on population growth has had a correspondingly positive impact on a region's wages, housing prices, rents, and cultural diversity. Similarly, the Brookings Institution reveals that immigration has a positive influence on metropolitan areas by reversing population losses, expanding the workforce, boosting home values, and reducing vacancy rates and foreclosures (Wilson and Singer 2011).

This chapter has two research objectives. The first is to understand the factors that contribute to the establishment of Latino neighborhoods in specific urban and suburban areas. The second is to explore how these Latino communities contribute to social, economic, and cultural resiliency in their neighborhoods. A three-part approach is used to address the research objectives and determine the influence that Latinos have on neighborhoods and cities. Part one looks at current changes in the demographic landscape and patterns of consumption. Part two explores the issues and topics relating to neighborhood selection based on the presence of sociocultural infrastructure and support. Part three examines in detail the physical aspects of urban composition and neighborhood structure. By better understanding the issues involved in each part of the creation of a Latino neighborhood, policy makers, civic leaders, urban planners, and designers can more effectively facilitate the development and growth of healthier urban Latino communities, contributing to the economic revitalization of derelict urban areas.

Theoretical Framework

Scholars have focused on the social and cultural implications of the growing Latino population in this country and its potential impacts on the dynamics of our built environment. Academic literature has noted the increasing presence and cultural contributions of Latinos in the development of American metropolises (Davis 2001; Delgado 2011; Diaz 2005; Diaz and Torres 2012; New America Alliance Institute 2014). Such literature demonstrates the emergence of new geographies and sociopolitical constructions in cities and regions (Malavé and Giordani 2014; Odem and Cantrell Lacy 2009; Valle and Torres 2000). Specific topics that define Latino urbanism include the appropriation and readaptation of physical space for new purposes based on cultural expression and the emergence of multiethnic coalitions. In the last fifteen years a number of books, edited volumes, and special issues of journals have provided comprehensive approaches to the study of Latino spaces (Arreola 2005; Diaz and Torres 2012; González 2017; Lara 2012b; Rios, Vasquez, and Miranda 2012); however, little of this research addresses the manner in which the principles of Latino urbanism contribute to the creation of a more sustainable urbanism and to the development of socially and culturally healthier communities. The literature synthesized and reviewed in chapter 2 examined Latino urbanism from historical, social, political, and economic perspectives to develop a framework for this chapter.

During the past twenty-five years there has been a movement in the field of urban planning and design to more actively *rethink* our entire concept of urban life to include perspectives on how we live, where we work, where we play and shop, and, most importantly, how we relate to each other as human beings. Whereas much of the post–World War II era of urban development in the United States was characterized by the sprawl patterns of low-density auto-dependent and land development models, the past ten years has witnessed the emergence of the concept of *sustainable urbanism* as a response to dissatisfaction with these models and as a new way of thinking about cities, urban life, and the environment in general. Sustainable urbanism holds the promise of enhancing the quality of life while minimizing any potential harm to the environment. The focus of sustainable urbanism has been on the creation and support of communities that are so well designed logistically that residents can easily and eagerly choose to meet their daily transportation needs by walking or through public transit (Farr 2012). There have been other movements with similar objectives, such as "smart growth," "new urbanism," "green architecture," and "green buildings," all fostered by the U.S. Green Building Council (USGBC) and Leadership in Energy and Environmental Design (LEED). These movements have been important stepping stones toward achieving more sustainable environments, but individually cannot meet the overall challenges facing urban America. Researchers and scholars agree that only a comprehensive effort, one that combines the various initiatives into a cooperative, can lead to a new framework for supporting an improved and sustainable urban lifestyle (Bohl 2000; Calthorpe 1994; Farr 2012; Gehl and Svarre 2013; Glaser 2012). Common objectives for urban communities among the initiatives include practical alternatives to automobile transportation, high-performance buildings and infrastructure, compactness and biophila (access to nature), easy access to healthy foods, and a socially and culturally appealing form of residential life. Several authors argue that key principles of Latino urbanism include and predate all of these objectives of urban sustainability (Arreola 2012; Diaz and Torres 2012; Gámez 2002; González 2017; Lara 2012b; Mendez 2005; Rojas 1991).

Urbanism among Latinos in the Southwest predates the entire construct of what planners and designers are claiming as smart growth and other new models of development to generate more sustainable urban lifestyles. The development patterns that have supported extensive social interaction among neighbors in southwestern Latino communities have been in practice since the late 1800s (Diaz and Torres 2012). The spaces where daily activities such as walking, shopping, working, recreation, gardening, and social interaction take place have always been central to cultural expression among Latinos (Arreola 2005; Diaz and Torres 2012; Gámez 2002; Lara 2012; Rojas 1991). The settlement and development patterns of Latinos in U.S. cities, in fact, largely explains the sustainability of their communities.

Immigration to American cities has been characterized by two distinct patterns of settlement. The first is associated with principally European immigrants of the nineteenth and early twentieth centuries and was based on the availability of low-cost housing in or near the city's center where most employment opportunities existed (Smith and Furuseth 2006). These factors intuitively promoted the development of inner-city residential districts, as people, when given the option, tend to live close to where they work. Such development characterized older American cities such as New York, Boston, Philadelphia, and Chicago, all of which were principal destinations for European immigrants. Once a particular ethnic group established itself in a given inner-city neighborhood, they would attract future immigrants of the same ethnicity by providing the new arrivals with the support and social networks necessary for successful assimilation. However, urban/suburban sprawl, which has characterized metropolitan development in the United States over the past sixty years, has meant job opportunities and affordable housing are no longer confined to city centers. Immigrants began bypassing inner cities and settling directly in suburbs (Smith and Furuseth 2006).

U.S. Census Bureau data for 1990 and 2000 indicate that minorities contributed disproportionately to population increase in all of the nation's largest metropolitan areas (Frey 2001), and in this disproportional contribution to population growth, Latinos are disproportionately represented. Census data also indicate that Latino populations are no longer confined to inner-city neighborhoods, but rather are increasingly adopting a settlement pattern termed "heterolocalism" (Zelinsky and Lee 1998). Under this model, it is argued, immigrants are no longer bound on arrival to settle in traditional immigrant enclaves, nor, in so doing, to forgo the ethnic networks and social capital these enclaves traditionally represented. Rather, spatial concentration is replaced by factors such as telecommunications, institutional community structures (e.g., churches, clubs, and associations), social media, and various Internet technologies. Consequently, ethnic groups living throughout a city or region can effectively maintain the strong connections and common identity that is vital for new immigrants (Zelinsky and Lee 1998). This phenomenon has been observable among Latino immigrant communities over at least the past twenty-five years.

Several aspects of Latino urbanism have been linked to sustainable practices.

WALKABILITY

Walking is a central social practice in Latino communities that involves both communal learning and the engagement of others in a communally oriented cultural arena. It provides a face-to-face interaction that celebrates and energizes cultural solidarity (Diaz and Torres 2012). Walkability increases uses and activities in a given space or place. To walk through a place is to employ the senses of sight, hearing, touch, and smell to activate the process of memory association crucial in placemaking. Activities that occur in a place—friendly social interactions, free public concerts, community art shows, and more—are the basic building blocks of placemaking. These activities are why individuals initially come to place, as well as why they return.

USE OF PUBLIC TRANSIT

Immigrants in the United States today are more likely to walk, bicycle, carpool, and to use public transit to and from work and within their neighborhoods than are nonimmigrants. This pattern is statistically present even after controlling for a variety of demographic, socioeconomic, and spatial characteristics (Barajas, Chatman, and Weinstein 2016). Studies undertaken by the Pew Research Center show that Americans who are lower income, black or Latino, over fifty years of age, and who are immigrants are disproportionately likely to avail themselves of public transportation on a regular basis. Among urban residents, 34 percent of blacks and 27 percent of Latinos report taking public transit daily or weekly versus only 14 percent of whites. Foreign-born urban residents are more likely than urban dwellers native to the United States to regularly use public transportation as well (38 percent vs. 18 percent) (Anderson 2016). Part of the reason of why Latino immigrants are disproportionate users of public transit is that they are more likely than native-born Americans overall to reside in large metropolitan areas, areas where there tend to be more public transit options. Latino immigrants are also less likely to have access to an automobile than other groups and are therefore more likely to use public transit for commuting to and from work. Latinos also tend to live farther away from their jobs (Anderson 2016). The findings of the Pew Research Center support the concept of heterolocalism presented earlier, one in which recent' Latino immigrants are settling in suburban areas close to corridors that provide public transit to and from jobs.

COMMERCE AND ACCESS TO FRESH FOOD

Commercial establishments in Latino immigrant neighborhoods are a central part of daily life among residents. Residents depend largely, if not solely, on local ethnic supermarkets, grocery stores, and retail outlets for comestibles and other household needs. In many cases, this is because they lack private transportation or have limited access to public transit. The benefits that ethnic grocery stores and related businesses provide to immigrant neighborhoods have received little attention from urban researchers; however, for most Latino immigrant residents, direct access to culturally friendly commercial establishments is one of their neighborhood's most important spatial amenities. It is through these businesses that residents come to know their community, build relationships of trust and loyalty with business operators, and establish a humane way of conducting everyday routines in a culturally familiar manner (Diaz and Torres 2012). Ethnic grocery stores not only offer shoppers specialized products, but can enhance the appeal of an urban neighborhood as well. Such ethnic entrepreneurships tend to be heavily concentrated in neighborhoods with large immigrant populations (Largent, Schulz, and Schwieterman 2013). Studies have shown that low-income neighborhoods with large immigrant populations often enjoy a higher level of "food security" than do other poor communities in the United States, thanks largely to the freshness of fruits, meats, and vegetables available and to the pride and responsibility ethnic entrepreneurs take in their work (Khojasteh and Raja 2016; Largent, Schulz, and Schwieterman 1993). Latino small businesses also provide social, economic, and cultural comfort to their respective communities.

BIOPHILIA (ACCESS TO OPEN SPACE)

Access to open space and recreational facilities is an important aspect of urban life for Latino communities. Studies have shown that Latinos spend more time in public parks than do either whites or blacks (Loukaitou-Sideris 1995), something attributable to a Latino penchant for social activities over the solitary activities (such as jogging) often favored by other groups. Latinos do not use parks only for sports, but for relaxation, social occasions, fiestas, and entertainment events. Such use may involve large crowds and the preparation of large quantities of food. Latinos also take advantage of the opportunities that parks afford for gardening. The upkeep and maintenance of urban gardens provides a break from the hurried pace of urban life while also contributing to the community's social life (Diaz and Torres 2012; Stephens 2008).

To address the research objectives, this chapter explores a series of commercial corridor case studies at various scales and in different urban areas across the United States in order to learn from best practices and to draw out some lessons on cultural, social, and economic resiliency from immigrant neighborhoods. Resiliency is a concept found in all case study areas. It is not only the capacity for change but an ability to adapt without losing culture, community ties, and local traditions that can make a place home. The main focus of the case studies is on the extraordinary changes taking place in these corridors and neighborhoods that simultaneously contribute to the creation of more dynamic and economically viable communities. The study areas represent communities that have been transformed from derelict if not altogether abandoned neighborhoods to bustling and dynamic ethnic business and retail corridors. These cases give public policy makers, academics, and business owners examples of how Latino communities can revitalize retail corridors and improve both the local economy and overall quality of life. The steps that planners and policy makers can take to encourage this type of growth include responding to an urban population's increasing diversity and changing demands, examining the processes and mechanisms that contribute to ethno-cultural alienation in Latino neighborhoods, and ensuring that any revitalization efforts in Latino communities will enhance local assets. The case studies include the McDowell Corridor in Phoenix, Arizona; West Vernor–Bagley in Detroit, Michigan; the Morse Road Corridor and Sullivant Avenue in Columbus, Ohio; and West Washington Street in Indianapolis, Indiana.

The study areas are all currently evolving into vibrant commercial centers, centers that help to maintain social networks providing ties to native Latin American countries while working to acclimate new immigrants. A detailed analysis of business activities and census data in these case studies illustrates changing spatial patterns and demonstrates how ethnic minority entrepreneurs are giving new meaning to abandoned and/or derelict landscapes such as strip malls and older, economically depressed neighborhoods. An evaluation of the local conditions and threshold elements in the study areas (density, accessibility, safety, existing retail space, potential capacity building) can contribute to the level of success in the revitalization process. This chapter also explores the specific ways in which urban spaces are being transformed and modified to suit the needs and cultural preferences of their residents.

As cities and urban centers in the United States become more ethnically diverse, ethnic minorities will have a greater impact on the urban landscape and land-use patterns. Under current conditions, the revitalization and transformation of neighborhoods present challenges and barriers for planners, designers, and other individuals who promote policies and services that address local needs. Currently, and true of the case studies presented here, there is a lack of public policy and discussion about the role of immigration in revitalization, a lack of meaningful networks of communication between cities and their immigrant populations, and a lack of any formal process to facilitate redevelopment of vacant or neglected properties in areas ripe for revitalization. A better understanding of the needs and challenges facing the Latino community today can enable urban planning and design practice to provide place-based solutions that will best serve this population in the future.

Four Case Studies

PHOENIX, ARIZONA: THE MCDOWELL CORRIDOR

Context and Background

Phoenix has experienced a dramatic increase in its Latino population since the 1990s. As a result, demand for products and services tailored to this immigrant population has surged, and many businesses have opened to accommodate the influx of Latinos and their purchasing

Figure 7. The McDowell Corridor is located northeast of downtown Phoenix. Image by author.

power. In the emerging Latino neighborhoods, visible changes in the retail landscape are often one of the few outward clues to this rapid ethnic transformation (Oberle 2006, 149). One of the purposes of this study is to examine how commercial establishments and small businesses reflect the increasing impacts of Latino culture in an area and how they contribute to the social, economic, and cultural revitalization of underserved and depressed urban areas.

The McDowell Corridor is a blue-collar immigrant community in central Phoenix. The corridor's transformation from a decaying commercial area to a bustling retail and ethnic minority business center has played a crucial role in central Phoenix's growth and transformation.

During the 1970s, the McDowell Corridor was a suburban commercial corridor that housed some retail and service industries. However, the introduction of air-conditioned shopping malls in the 1970s and 1980s, such as the Metrocenter complex in northwest Phoenix in 1972, the Paradise Valley Mall in northeastern Phoenix in 1979, the Desert Sky Mall in west Phoenix in 1981, and the Fiesta Mall shopping center in the city of Mesa, east of Phoenix, in 1979, led to the closing of most local retail and commercial businesses. Following the successful opening of the Metrocenter, the city's planning department decided to become a more active participant in planning the location of such major retail centers. With the objective of more evenly distributing economic growth and employment opportunities, the city of Phoenix adopted an official growth policy— "the urban village concept"—in 1974 (Gammage 1996, 56). Under this plan, the city was divided into nine villages; each village contained a village core and a regional shopping and employment plan. The urban village plan was primarily useful in providing Phoenix with a means of geographically organizing a large city into manageable units. It was also a rationale to support additional shopping centers (Gammage 2003, 158).

As a result of the implementation of the urban village plan, in which growth and development were directed to strategic areas throughout the city, abandoned commercial units became commonplace along the McDowell Corridor. The Latino population boom of the 1990s and the resulting demand for specific products and services initiated this area's transformation into a viable commercial corridor based on cultural entrepreneurship. Latino immigrants, who operate roughly 75 percent of the businesses in the area, are contributing to the area's revitalization. Businesses in the McDowell Corridor include mainly Mexican- and Central American-owned restaurants, bakeries, grocery stores, gasoline stations, travel agencies, hair salons, and auto-related services, as well as blocks of strip malls that house diverse specialty stores. There is now general satisfaction with the level of retail service the community is receiving.

Analysis of the Local Conditions and Presence of Threshold Elements in the McDowell Corridor

1. *Density:* The corridor is approximately 1.5 miles from downtown Phoenix and is surrounded by residential areas. The corridor can sustain commercial activity at the levels of both a neighborhood center and neighborhood subcenter, given its diverse type of businesses and the community it serves. The density of the area is 8,085 people per square mile, which meets the ideal minimum household density (5,000 people per square mile) for convenience markets surrounding a targeted corridor.

2. *Accessibility:* The corridor is easily accessible by both car and public transit. McDowell Road is a major east-west artery in the

metropolitan area, and the corridor is adjacent to three major freeways (I-10, I-17, and State Route 202) that provide access to the entire metropolitan area.

3. *Safety:* The perception of safety is positive in the area, confirmed during informal interviews with business owners and local residents. Throughout the area there is excellent lighting, continuous sidewalks, and ample street amenities.

4. *Existing Retail:* The corridor has a diverse mix of retail businesses concentrated around four major commercial nodes. Each node is anchored by at least one large store, accompanied by smaller stores and restaurants. Many of the businesses have been in operation for ten to fifteen years. The corridor is in a general state of redevelopment, given the evolving nature of the local economy and of the Latino population.

5. *Capacity Building:* Support for economic activity has been limited to a small number of local nonprofit organizations, including the Arizona Hispanic Chamber of Commerce, the Arizona Community Foundation, Latino Unidos, the National Latina/ Latino Commission, and Fuerza Local (which launched a business accelerator program in 2013).

Other sites throughout Phoenix are undergoing similar transformations, including West Van Buren Street, South Central Avenue, and Grand Avenue in central Phoenix. Most of these sites are located in declining and dilapidated areas, where the revitalization is usually undertaken by Latino immigrants. While transformations are occurring throughout Phoenix, this case study focuses on a one-and-a-half-mile section west of the McDowell Corridor, between Seventeenth Street and Thirty-Second Street (Oberle 2006, 149). McDowell Corridor was selected over other sites because it is the most transitional and has the fastest-growing Latino population in the metropolitan area. It is strategically located between existing "Latino cores," one located where Interstates 10 and 17 intersect, the other the Garfield neighborhood to the south. The study area is located in the "Latino fringe" districts, which are in the vanguard of the demographic shift (Arreola 2005, 15; Oberle 2006, 154). The Latino population in these districts doubled between 1990 and 2000, and it continues to increase.

Figure 8. Examples of vernacular expression along the McDowell Corridor signal the presence of immigrant groups in the area. Photos by author.

Demographic Trends and Impacts

Cities throughout the Southwest have experienced significant urban demographic change. Immigration and natural growth have impacted major metropolitan areas in the region. According to the U.S. Census, the Latino population made up 16 percent of Arizona's population in 1970, 18.8 percent in 1990, and 25.3 percent in 2000. The Center for Competitiveness and Prosperity Research reported that Arizona had the fastest-growing Latino population in the nation, increasing

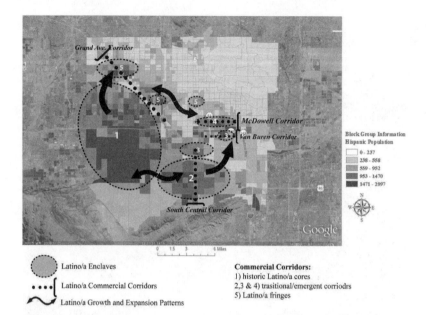

Figure 9. This diagram highlights the Latino commercial corridors in Phoenix, including Latino cores, transitional and emerging corridors, and Latino fringes, which are constantly redefining the new cultural geography in the Phoenix metropolitan region. Image by author.

12 percent between July 2000 and July 2002 alone. Moreover, the Latino share of Arizona's total population rose from 25 percent to just under 30 percent between 2000 and 2010 (Rex 2011). The Pew Hispanic Center notes that Arizona's Latino population of 1.9 million in 2011 was the sixth-largest in the nation, behind only California, Texas, Florida, New York, and Illinois. Analysts agree, however, that recent growth has been slower than some studies had projected. Tough economic times coupled with restrictions on undocumented immigrant workers are probably responsible for discouraging some potential immigrants (Lacey 2010). Led by a 46 percent increase in its Latino population, Arizona's overall population rose from 5.1 million to 6.4 million over the past decade, a rate second only to Nevada's. In statewide terms, Mohave County saw a 501 percent increase in its Latino population over the past twenty years, the largest increase of any in the state. Maricopa County, in which Phoenix is located, had the largest increase in absolute terms, adding more than 780,000

Latinos (a 48 percent increase). Latinos there now make up 30 percent of the entire population. The white population in Maricopa County increased during this period as well, but by merely 10 percent. Demographers expect the Latino population will continue to rise by a percentage point every two or three years.

A sign of the changing demographics in Arizona is evident in the most popular names for children in the state, such as Isabella and Sophia for girls and Angel for boys. Of the Latino population in the state, nearly 40 percent is under the age of eighteen. The youthfulness of this population, when coupled with untold older Latinos legally unable to vote, translates into enormous unrealized political clout (Lacey 2010).

The popular image of Arizona as a state of white retirees is quickly being dispelled. Given its current demography and age distribution, Arizona is not an old, white person's state. Rather, its age distribution is very close to the national average.

The disproportionate presence of the Latino community is undeniable and will remain so in spite of the tone of current legislation. One example of such legislation is Arizona Senate Bill 1070, often referred to simply as Arizona S.B. 1070. The Arizona law makes it a misdemeanor for an alien to be found in Arizona without carrying required documents and further requires that state law enforcement officials attempt to determine an individual's immigration status during a "lawful stop, detention or arrest" or during a "lawful contact" not specific to any activity when there is reasonable suspicion that the individual is an illegal immigrant. The fervor in Arizona against illegal immigration is so intense that politicians have pushed some of the nation's toughest laws regarding illegal immigration, while citizen activists have taken to patrolling the border themselves (Lacey 2010).

Phoenix's demographic trends will likely impact the state's socioeconomic development in all sectors. Arizona is experiencing significant demographic shifts, with a population increase of approximately 25 percent between 2000 and 2010. It now stands at a turning point demographically: 42 percent of the state's population is nonwhite, the Latino share alone making up 30 percent. Already people of color are the majority in four U.S. states, and in Arizona where, as in nine other states, they make up somewhere between 40 and 50 percent of the total population, they are poised to make it too a "minority-majority

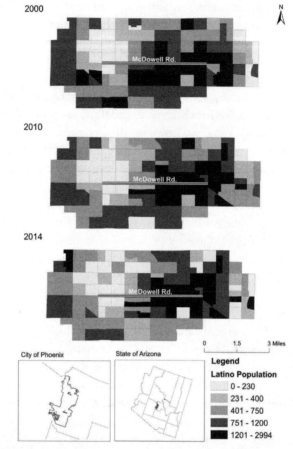

Scale	Name	2000			2010			2014			Percent Change (%, '00 – '14)	
		Total Pop	Latino Pop	%	Total Pop	Latino Pop	%	Total Pop	Latino Pop	%	Total Pop	Latino Pop
State	Arizona	5,130,632	1,295,617	25.3	6,392,017	1,895,149	29.6	6,561,516	1,977,026	30.1	27.9	**52.6**
County	Maricopa	3,072,149	763,341	24.8	3,817,117	1,128,741	29.6	3,947,382	1,181,100	29.9	28.5	**54.7**
Corridor	McDowell Rd.	158,618	88,006	55.5	144,361	78,357	54.3	143,754	72,918	50.7	-9.4	**-17.1**

Note) *For Data Source and Boundary Selection, Refer to Appendix.

Figure 10. Latino population change in the McDowell Corridor. Between 2000 and 2014 the Latino population in the McDowell Corridor decreased by 17.1 percent, due in part to legislation of a discriminatory nature. One example of such legislation is Arizona Senate Bill 1070, often referred to simply as Arizona S.B. 1070. Image by author.

state" (Cardenas, Kerby, and Wilf 2012). In addition, Arizona has one of the largest age/ethnicity disparities in the United States. Whereas in 2010, 80 percent of all American seniors there were white, only 54 percent of state's youth were white. In fact, of those between the ages of five and seventeen, 26.3 percent were Latino and 21.2 percent African American (Cardenas, Kerby, and Wilf 2012). Though Latinos were only 9 percent of the electorate in 2008, these statistics indicate that figure will soon rise dramatically. The increase in the Latino population will soon translate into political power. In 2008 Latinos were 9 percent of the voting electorate. The pressure to turn those numbers into political power is only increasing, as the Latino share of the electorate reached 18 percent of all eligible voters in the state in 2010. As Latinos become the majority of the population in both Arizona and Phoenix, their characteristics, lifestyles, and decisions will dramatically alter the physical and cultural landscapes of both the state and the city.

Economic Trends and Impacts

Unlike other cities in the Southwest, such as Tucson, Albuquerque, and El Paso, where Spanish and Mexican traditions date back hundreds of years, Phoenix is a relatively new metropolitan area that was largely dependent on migration from the U.S. Midwest and East for its initial growth. It expanded greatly during the economic boom of the 1990s. The Latino population in Phoenix has grown three times faster than the non-Latino population during the last few years, a dynamic that has resulted in unprecedented economic purchasing power. Arizona currently ranks seventh largest among U.S. states in terms of Latino buying power ($31 billion, which is up from $17.5 billion in 2003) (Humphreys 2008). Latinos are playing an important role in the six steps of the urban cycle there, a cycle consisting of the following phases: construction, abandonment, conversion, abandonment, demolition, and new construction. Every city goes through this cycle. Sometimes the cycle skips a phase, but the essential motion persists (Kyvig and Marty 2000). The McDowell Corridor is currently going through a conversion phase, as evidenced by the Latino creation of new forms of public urban spaces as well as their reappropriation of spaces for their own uses.

The Latino cultural scene in the Phoenix metropolitan area has also grown rapidly. Once thought of as a weak market for Latino entertainment by organizers of sports and concerts, Phoenix has now become a routine stop for popular Latino musicians and pop artists, as well as international sports teams, including soccer teams from Latin America and Spain. Upscale Scottsdale, renowned for its golf links and health spas, now also hosts two Latino nightclubs, and a new demand for Latino theater is emerging where none existed before. The *Las Vegas Sun* has further reported that in the past fifteen years about fifty Latino-owned restaurants have opened in Arizona (Carlie 1997). These are examples of the cultural shift taking place beyond the McDowell Corridor.

Their growing population has contributed to the increase of purchasing power among Latinos, with Latino spending power in Arizona surpassing the $27 billion annual mark. In 2008, *AzBusiness* magazine reported that "Latinos are now regarded as indispensable to the success of every major economic sector in Arizona" (Harris 2008). Further evidence of this power comes from a 2008 study by the University of Georgia's Selig Center for Economic Growth, which indicates that total U.S. Latino purchasing power totaled $863.1 billion in 2007 and is growing by $1 billion every six weeks. At this rate, it is estimated that it will reach $1.2 trillion by end of 2010 (Humphreys 2008, 10). The U.S. Bureau of Economic Analysis estimates that this rate of growth is nearly three times that for the nation as a whole over the past decade (Humphreys 2008, 11).

The McDowell Corridor's businesses reflect the state's Latino spending trends. A 2010 inventory of the existing businesses in the McDowell Corridor revealed four distinct commercial nodes based on the type and physical distribution of businesses along the corridor. The inventory distinguished three types of businesses: (1) clothing for special occasions (bridal accessories, custom-made alterations); (2) auto-related businesses (auto repair, window tinting, stereos and car alarms, used tire shops, and parts and services); and (3) groceries/dining (chain markets, specialty food and products, fish and meats, and ethnic restaurants).

Summary and Implications for Future Planning

Latino business entrepreneurs along the McDowell Corridor were interviewed both on a drop-in basis and through introductions from other business owners in the area with the intent of gathering

Figure 11. Examples of adaptive use are common sights along the McDowell Corridor, contributing to the urban cycle in which abandoned infrastructure finds new uses. Some examples include a former gas station converted into a car wash and an obsolete commercial building partitioned and converted into several ethnic-oriented businesses. Photos by author.

information about the development of businesses, customer profiles, and identification of customer needs. At the time of the survey there were ninety-eight Latino-oriented businesses in the study area, and 75 percent of the businesses were Latino owned. Efforts were made to interview a sample of business owners who represented the types of businesses listed in table 3.1. Business owners

Figure 12. There are four defined commercial nodes based on type and number of businesses along the McDowell Corridor. Images and photos by author.

were asked about their backgrounds, migration histories, employees, and property and business operations. The interviews provided insights into why immigrants are selecting McDowell Corridor as a location for their investments, as well as how they are contributing to the local economy and impacting the built environment in their communities.

Owing to the ethnically oriented, small-business nature of the commercial corridor along McDowell, the majority of the Latino entrepreneurs interviewed for this study operate "mom and pop" types of retail and service establishments. The interviews with individual entrepreneurs were supplemented by interviews with local immigrant business leaders to provide a broad perspective on issues faced by Phoenix's immigrants.

Seven out of sixteen of the interviewed entrepreneurs started their businesses out of abandoned or vacant properties, most of which required some minor upgrades before they were fully functional. All of the business owners invested in improving their properties. In some cases, a single property was subdivided into two or three individual businesses, as in the case of the Yerberia Guadalupe and the barbershop on the southwest part of the corridor. In other cases, a single business has grown and occupied two different buildings in order to accommodate its needs, which is what happened with the Dulceria Pico Rico. Similar cases can be found throughout the corridor. Only two of the businesses are located in properties that were in more or less fair condition to begin with.

Table 1. Phoenix, Arizona, McDowell Corridor ranking of businesses in the area based on quantity and type during the interview and inventory process.

Ranking	Type of business	Representative businesses
1	Special occasion clothing (bridal shop)	Esthela's, Bella's Closet, Lupita's Fashion, Ofelia's, Da Paul
2	Ethnic food and markets (mercados latinos)	El Caporal, Safari Market, Food City, La Plaza 2000, Mercado Latino, Tienda Centroamericana, Fantacia
3	Auto-related services (wheels, stereo parts, and services)	The Wheel Shop, Monte Vista, Median, Arellanos Tire, JDM Auto, Moises, Jalisco Tire, Estereos y Alarmas, Alejandro's
4	Entertainment (nightclubs and bars)	Delirium, Karamba, Aqua, Kitty's, Boom, El Zarape, Furia Musical
5	Ethnic restaurant and food services	Guanaquito, Tacos Mich, Filiberto's, Playa Del Sol, San Carlos, El Ranchero, Tacos Chiwas, Rosita's, La Barquita, Tortas Paquime, Guerrerence, Dalia's
6	Specific products and services (yerberias, fiestas, dulcerias)	Yedy's Beauty, Las Brisas, Gracie, Importaciones Valentina, Botas El Jibaro

Ranking	Other businesses that have taken notice of the Latino market in the area
1	Miscellaneous stores (Checker Auto Parts, Pep Boys, Payless Shoe Source, Thrift Store)
2	Miscellaneous services (check cashing, dollar store, money wiring)

While half of the interviewed business owners cited a need to upgrade their properties, none of them had been able to obtain bank loans to begin their business operations. Most of them relied on informal lending systems such as friends and family to supplement their savings and allow them to invest in their businesses.

The most important reason given for establishing a business in the area was the presence of family, friends, and other people with similar backgrounds. Many also noted that the McDowell Corridor, and Phoenix in general, is attractive because property ownership there is affordable. Six of the sixteen entrepreneurs interviewed had moved directly to Phoenix from Mexico, El Salvador, or Ecuador, while four business operators had resided in the United States before moving to

Phoenix. Among the latter group, the operators had moved mainly from Southern and Northern California. Most of the businesses had hired two to four employees, with a mix of full-time and part-time staffers. Most hiring was done through family and friends.

In the last twenty-five years, much of the attention in city planning and design in Phoenix has focused on downtown revitalization and suburban development. There are also other informal revitalization efforts taking place within the city's boundaries as a reaction to "benign neglect" from city officials. Like many other cities, Phoenix overestimated the amount of retail trade that would occur during the 1980s and 1990s, creating a gap during which demand had to catch up with development. As a consequence, the McDowell Corridor was saddled with vacant building stock that provided low rents and accessible locations for Latino entrepreneurs. Buildings were adapted for new commercial uses, enlivening street life. The changes were entirely responses to market demands and opportunities in a changing demographic landscape and are testimony to the important role that these businesses play in contributing to the social and economic vitality of their neighborhood. These efforts deserve academic and public attention and should inform future planning and design policy. The revitalization of the McDowell Corridor transpired without formal planning or programmed design. If the city had pursued to its logical conclusion its predetermined multi-nucleic model or urban village plan, McDowell Corridor might have been redesigned as a mere passageway through prescribed centers. In other words, the kind of intervention promoted in comprehensive planning might have made things worse, not better. In places such as the McDowell Corridor, planners should work incrementally if they do comprehensive planning.

DETROIT, MICHIGAN: THE WEST VERNOR–BAGLEY STREET CORRIDOR 1

Context and Background

The West Vernor–Bagley Street Corridor of Mexicantown is located in southwest Detroit and encompasses approximately fifteen square

1. Note: Parts of an earlier version of this case study were published in an article in *Journal of Urbanism*.

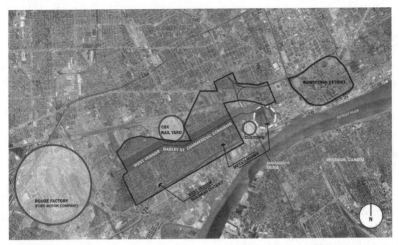

Figure 13. The West Vernor–Bagley Street Corridor site context, showing the study area and physical barriers created by the freeways and major manufacturing centers. Image by author.

miles. It is bordered on the west by the city of Dearborn, Michigan; on the north by Interstate 94; on the east by the M-10 and downtown Detroit; and on the south by the Detroit River, which separates Detroit from the Canadian city of Windsor, Ontario. Southwest Detroit has long been a home to immigrants—first from Ireland, then from Poland, Lebanon, Italy, and from the U.S. South. More recently, immigrants have come from Mexico and other Latin American countries. Today, the neighborhood's population is about 50 percent Hispanic, and almost half of the business community is Hispanic as well (ULI 2013).

The Latino population in Detroit has more than doubled in the past ten years. Latinos have been present in Detroit since the 1920s, but large numbers of Latino immigrants began moving to Mexicantown in the 1990s, and the numbers continue to rise. According to a study done by Erickson (2007), there are around four hundred thousand Latinos in Michigan, half of whom live in Detroit. The study neighborhood is located in southwest Detroit in the shadow of the Ambassador Bridge, a busy border crossing between the United States and Canada. It is an unusual neighborhood in that it is unlike most of Detroit, which is largely characterized by vacant lots, abandoned buildings, a declining urban population, chronically high unemployment, and high crime rates. Rather, in the West Vernor–Bagley Street Corridor and Mexicantown there are beautiful homes, manicured lawns, an increasing population, thriving small businesses, and a lively street life. The area has been going through different stages of the urban cycle, from construction to abandonment to reappropriation, since the early 1990s, but within the last twenty years the transformation process has become more persistent (*Hispanic Population* 2008, 9–10). Sadly, the area is sandwiched between I-75 and some of Michigan's largest industrial plants. It and its surroundings constitute some of Michigan's "most polluted zip codes," according to an analysis by University of Michigan environmental scientists (Oosting 2010). In fact, the area comprising Mexicantown's zip code of 48217 and that of its neighbors—home to both working-class neighborhoods and such industrial sites as the Marathon Oil Refinery and several asphalt plants—account for six of the ten most polluted zip codes in the state (Oosting 2010). The area has also been bisected by expansion plans of Detroit's central business district and the addition of a freeway through the city (Alvarado 2003).

With all of its existing challenges and opportunities, the West Vernor–Bagley Street Corridor is an example of neighborhood revitalization through ethnic economic entrepreneurship. The local retail sector has been revitalized and provides a model on how to improve both the economy and quality of life of a public realm for its residents and visitors. A detailed analysis of business activities and census data with respect to the corridor shows changing spatial patterns and demonstrates how ethnic minority entrepreneurs are creating neighborhoods and giving new meaning to abandoned, unmaintained urban infrastructure. This case study also investigates the specific ways in which urban spaces are being transformed and modified to suit the needs and cultural preferences of their residents.

Detroit, and southeast Michigan in general, has experienced a dramatic increase in Latino population since the 1990s. As a result, demand for products and services tailored to this immigrant group has skyrocketed, with many businesses opening to accommodate the increasing purchasing power of Latinos. In the emerging Latino neighborhoods, visible changes in the retail landscape are often the only outward clues of this rapid ethnic transformation (Kaplan and

Li 2006). One of the purposes of this case study is to examine how commercial establishments and small businesses can contribute to the creation of neighborhoods while promoting the social, economic, and cultural revitalization of underserved and/or economically depressed urban areas.

The Latino population boom of the 1990s and the consequent demands for specific products and services fostered the West Vernor–Bagley Street area's transformation into a neighborhood with a viable commercial corridor based on cultural entrepreneurships. The study area includes two local neighborhoods, the West Vernor Business District and Mexicantown. According to the Southwest Detroit Business Association, both are among Detroit's most pedestrian-friendly communities. Latino immigrants, who operate roughly 85 percent of the businesses in the area, are contributing to the area's revitalization. Businesses in the corridor include mainly Mexican- and Central American-owned restaurants, bakeries, grocery stores, gasoline stations, travel agencies, hair salons, and auto-related services, as well as blocks of strip malls that house diverse specialty stores. The area helps serve the needs of its community.

While other sites throughout southeastern Michigan, including Pontiac and Dearborn, are undergoing similar transformations, this case study focuses on a three-and-a-half-mile section of the West Vernor–Bagley Street Corridor, between Eighteenth Street and Woodmere Street. The rationale for selecting this area over other sites is that it has one of the fastest-growing Latino populations in the Detroit metropolitan area. The Latino population there doubled between 1990 and 2000, and it continues to increase. The corridor is strategically located between major transportation and employment centers and a busy border crossing between the United States and Canada.

Analysis of Local Conditions and the Presence of Threshold Elements in the West Vernor–Bagley Street Corridor

1. *Density*: The corridor is located 1.5 miles southwest of downtown Detroit. Its location provides excellent access to other services and infrastructure. Given the level of commercial activity and the diverse mix of businesses, specialty restaurants, and entertainment venues, the corridor is considered both a neighborhood

center and a specialty center. The area has a density of 5,733 people per square mile and so meets the ideal minimum household density (5,000 people per square mile) for convenience markets surrounding a targeted corridor.

2. *Accessibility:* The area is considered both a pedestrian- and transit-oriented corridor and is accessible by both car and public transportation. West Vernor is a major access point to downtown Detroit and is categorized as a highway. The I-75 and I-96 freeways provide access to the rest of the city. This neighborhood has access to the Ambassador Bridge, which connects the United States with Canada.

3. *Safety:* There is a very positive perception of safety in the area, one confirmed through informal interviews with local business owners and residents. The area enjoys good lighting, continuous sidewalks, and street amenities that promote pedestrian activities.

4. *Existing Retail:* The economically stable corridor features a concentration of diverse and fully operating retail establishments and other businesses, some of which (including several well-known restaurants) are generations old.

5. *Capacity Building:* The long-standing Latino residential and business community receives extensive and effective support from nonprofit organizations who actively market their services. The University of Michigan has compiled a comprehensive list of resources available to Latino families in southwest Michigan, including general community resources, social services, immigration and legal resources, adult education and job training, youth support, and professional mentoring.

Demographic Trends and Impacts

Cities throughout the country have experienced significant urban demographic change as immigration and natural growth have impacted them. According to the 2006 U.S. Census, the Latino population in Michigan increased by 60.7 percent between 1990 and 2000, while Michigan's total population increased by only 6.9 percent during the same time frame. The Latino population is projected to make up 24.4 percent of Michigan's population by the year 2050. In 1990, Latinos accounted for 1.9 percent of the total population of southeastern Michigan. By 2000, they accounted for 2.8 percent, an increase of 44.5 percent. Michigan has more Latinos than most other states, ranking fifteenth (Alvarado 2003, 59). Likewise, Detroit has been transformed by an influx of Latino immigrants to the region—from 2000 to 2007, the Latino population of the Detroit area grew 28 percent—spurring an estimated $200 million of investment in homes and retail developments (Ghosh 2010). These trends in population growth will likely impact the state's socioeconomic development in all sectors. As the Latino population increases, its characteristics, lifestyles, and decisions will dramatically alter the physical and cultural landscapes of both the state of Michigan and the city of Detroit. Demographers have attributed the increase in the Latino population to better wages and schools, a chance to gain a college education for their children, a chance to start small businesses, or to family members already established in the area whom immigrants wished to join (Cohen, Passel, and Lopez 2011).

Economic Trends and Impacts

The Latino population in southwest Detroit has grown three times faster than the non-Latino population during the last few years, a dynamic that has resulted in unprecedented economic purchasing power. The earnings of Latinos and the spin-off jobs that they support amounted to $10.2 billion in 2006, with economic activity adding $14.5 billion to the 2006 gross regional product in southeast Michigan (Erickson 2007; *Hispanic Population* 2008; Kayitsigna 2007). This economic activity generated $727 million in state government tax revenue in 2006 (*Hispanic Population* 2008). Latinos are contributing to the economic urban cycle—that is, construction, abandonment, conversion, abandonment, demolition, and new construction. The West Vernor–Bagley Street Corridor is currently going through a conversion phase, as evidenced by the Latino creation of new forms of public urban spaces and reappropriation of abandoned spaces for their own uses.

By the end of the 1920s, Mexicans and Mexican Americans in Detroit were able to secure employment and find places to live, and were well on their way to establishing themselves as another ethnic group in the city (Alvarado 2003, 16). Residents in southwest Detroit established more than twenty Mexican and Mexican American

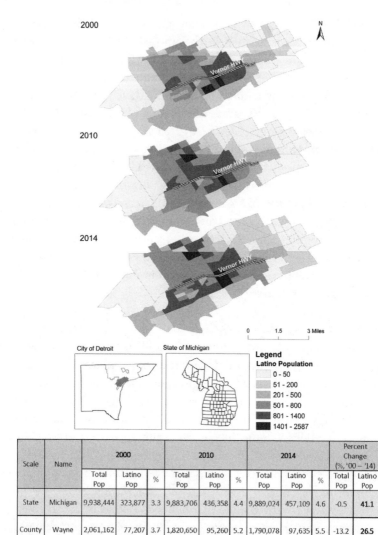

Scale	Name	2000			2010			2014			Percent Change (%, '00 – '14)	
		Total Pop	Latino Pop	%	Total Pop	Latino Pop	%	Total Pop	Latino Pop	%	Total Pop	Latino Pop
State	Michigan	9,938,444	323,877	3.3	9,883,706	436,358	4.4	9,889,024	457,109	4.6	-0.5	41.1
County	Wayne	2,061,162	77,207	3.7	1,820,650	95,260	5.2	1,790,078	97,635	5.5	-13.2	26.5
Corridor	Vernor Hwy.	97,360	35,490	36.5	83,603	37,117	44.4	83,320	39,936	47.9	-14.4	12.5

Note) *For Data Source and Boundary Selection, Refer to Appendix.

Figure 14. Latino population change within the West Vernor–Bagley Street Corridor compared to that of state and county. Between 2000 and 2010 in the West Vernor–Bagley Street Corridor the Latino population increased approximately 7.9 percent, whereas total population declined approximately 3.7 percent. In addition, the Latino proportion of the population in the study area (63.9 percent in 2000 and 71.6 percent in 2010) is substantially higher than that at the state and county levels, which ranges between 3.26 percent and 4.97 percent. Image by author.

Figure 15. Community anchors/support networks (church, park, store, and community center). The typical community anchors in the study area are found grouped together in three different locations along the corridor. Image by author.

fraternal organizations, which constituted mutual aid societies and cultural organizations for the preservation and improvement of Mexican and Mexican American culture (Alvarado 2003). One of these early fraternities was Las Casas de Asistencias (Homes of Assistance), which provided rooms and hot meals for single men. Others included the Mexican Catholic Society, the Latin American Club, Circulo Mutualista Mexicano (Mexican Mutual Aid Circle), Centro Cultura (Cultural Center), Los Obreros Unidos Mexicanos (United Mexican Workers), and El Club Artístico Femenino (Ladies Artistic Club). In the 1920s, the Ford Motor Company established the Ford Sociological Department, the primary function of which was to provide social and cultural activities for Latin American employees.

Since the 1920s, residents in the area have received help from the Catholic Church, which has a strong presence in the community. The Catholic Church viewed its community work as an investment that would support future growth in the numbers of faithful (Vargas 1999, 70). In southwest Detroit and in areas along the West Vernor–Bagley Street Corridor, the church has taken special interest in promoting the well-being of immigrants arriving in the city. The Catholic churches in the area were first established to serve the European Catholic immigrants who settled there. Historically, Detroit's corporate leaders have considered Christian principles a defense against rampant socialist ideas that could imperil worker productivity (Vargas 1999, 71). The most important and influential of all the Mexican and Mexican American groups established in Detroit was VFW Mexican American Post #505, which was founded by Mexican American veterans of World War II (Alvarado 2003, 36).

Currently, most social and legal services for the Latino community in the area are provided by nonprofit organizations. Latin Americans for Social and Economic Development (LASED) and the Southwest Detroit Business Association (SWDBA) are two of the most active organizations in the area. LASED has assisted people of all ages with a variety of bilingual services, ranging from translation services to recreational activities for older adults to youth development programs. SWDBA provides support in areas of façade improvement, small-business technical assistance, and real estate development. There has also been an effort to encourage patronage of Latino-owned businesses by the Detroit branch of the NAACP through its "Buy in Detroit" program (Alvarado 2003, 60). In the 1960s, many Latino immigrants in Detroit began occupying working-class districts around Ford's River

Figure 16. Successful examples of adaptive uses in mixed-use development. Photos by author.

Rouge Plant, which had initially been the home of eastern and southern European immigrants at the turn of the century. Once these immigrants were established and had gained upward mobility, they moved out of the working-class districts located around the factories and automotive-related manufacturing industries.

In the West Vernor–Bagley Street Corridor, the transformation from run-down strip malls to a Latino cultural hub or Main Street is obvious on a daily basis, but it is particularly noticeable on weekends, when residents come out to do their shopping. On Saturdays and Sundays, the entire district is filled with the sounds and smells from the stores and restaurants along the street. These activities give the corridor an original identity and create a sense of place and character that is determined by its regular clientele and visitors. The businesses contribute to an active street life, where the elderly, children, and young adults mix in a neighborly fashion as they shop. The area has become a common area where people can relate to one another, promoting social cohesion and providing social and psychological support to individuals and communities. The indicators of the success of this corridor include the presence of successful business anchors—establishments in the area that provide neighborhood residents and visitors with goods and services at reasonable prices—and the creation of a culture of opportunity and success. These indicators and the consequent level of social and cultural activity they generate are not apparent in other neighborhoods around Detroit.

Summary and Implications for Future Planning

The methodology for this case parallels that of the previous case study in Phoenix, Arizona. Latino business entrepreneurs along the West Vernor–Bagley Street Corridor were interviewed both on a drop-in basis and through introductions from other business owners in the area in order to gather information about the development of businesses, customer profiles, and the nature of customer needs. At the time of the survey, there were 212 Latino-oriented businesses (85 percent of all businesses) in the study area. Efforts were made to interview a sample of business owners who represented all the types of businesses listed in table 3.2. Business owners were asked about their backgrounds, migration histories, employees, and property and business operations. The interviews provided insight into both why immigrants have been selecting the West Vernor–Bagley Street Corridor as a location for their investments and how they are contributing to the local economy and impacting the built environment in their community.

The majority of the Latino entrepreneurs interviewed for this study operate "mom and pop" types of retail and service

Table 2. Detroit, Michigan, West Vernor–Bagley Street Corridor ranking of businesses in the area based on quantity and type during the interview and inventory process.

Ranking	Type of business	Number of businesses by type	Representative businesses
1	Ethnic food and markets (mercados latinos)	52	La Colmena, Mexican Village, Los Galanes, Las Gloria Bakery, Lupita's, Xochimilco, Evie's, La Jalisciense, El Comal, Armando's, Mexican Town Bakery, La Michoacana, Taqueria El Rey, Brown's Bun Baking, Chilango's Bakery, La Hacienda, Taco Mexico, La Tropicana Market
2	Specialty products and services	26	Lupe's Barber Shop, El Guero's Barber Shop, Lupita's Ideal Beauty, Ave María Religious Shop, Twice as Nice Shop, Primaveras
3	Personal services (beauty shops, barber shops, natural medicine)	25	Lupita's Laundromat, Giovana's Lounge, Sisters Beauty Salon
4	Entertainment (bars, nightclubs)	19	El Club, VL Bar, Super Mexico, Coogan's Bar, El Rancho, La Terraza, Our Detroit
5	Social services and nonprofit organizations	16	LASED, All Saints Literacy Center, Southwest Housing Solutions, SW Solutions Adult Learning Center, WAY Academy, Compas Center, LASED Senior and Youth Center, El Centro Hispano News
6	Special-occasion shops	15	Percy's Gallery, Delia's, Seven Leguas Western Wear, MoneyGram, Dino's Travel, Soccer Store
7	Auto-related business	12	Audio City, Sanchez Auto, Certified Suspension
8	Miscellaneous	13	Metro Flea Market, La Fiesta, Donato Furniture, A & G Dollar

establishments. The interviews with individual entrepreneurs were supplemented by interviews with local immigrant business leaders and nonprofit organizations in the area, providing a broad perspective on issues faced by Michigan's immigrants. These organizations included the Southwest Detroit Business Association and Latin Americans for Social and Economic Development (LASED).

Eighteen of the twenty-four entrepreneurs interviewed started their businesses on abandoned or vacant properties, most of which required some minor upgrades in order to be fully functional. All of these business owners have invested in improving their businesses, some of them with support from the Southwest Detroit Business Association. In some cases, a single property was subdivided into two or three individual businesses, as in the case of Café con Leche and Guero's, a barbershop in the southwest corner of the corridor. In other cases, a single business has grown and occupied two different buildings in order to accommodate its needs, which is what happened with La Michoacana Tortilla Factory and Mexicantown Baker. Similar cases can be found throughout the corridor.

Half of the business owners interviewed needed to upgrade their properties, but although many of them sought bank loans, none were able to obtain them to begin business operations. Instead, most of them relied on informal lending sources such as friends and family to supplement their savings and allow them to invest in their businesses.

As was the case in the previous case study, the most common reason given for establishing a business in the area was the presence of family, friends, or other people with similar backgrounds. Many entrepreneurs also noted that the West Vernor–Bagley Street Corridor, and Detroit in general, was attractive because property ownership there is affordable. Fourteen of the twenty-four entrepreneurs moved to Detroit directly from Mexico, El Salvador, or Puerto Rico, while four had lived elsewhere in the United States before moving to Detroit. Of the latter group, most came from other areas of the Midwest and from the Southwest. Six of the twenty-four had been residents in the area for more than two generations. Most of the businesses hired two to four employees, with a mix of full-time and part-time staffers. Most hiring was done through family and friends.

This case study helps explain why Latino neighborhoods form in large urban areas and what factors and forces shape them. Latino communities have proven to be very resilient in adapting and forming urban neighborhoods that focus on people and place (Lara 2012b). Until very recently, virtually no official city planning efforts had been undertaken by Detroit since the 1960s, although such efforts had been made by community development and nonprofit organizations. This is a case in which the city had been absent in the process, but its neglect actually helped foster the vibrant, entrepreneurial life that now exists in the revitalized corridor. Given the conditions in the West Vernor–Begley Street Corridor before its rejuvenation, one of the lessons for planners and designers in this case is that prescriptive planning and design systems do not always yield positive outcomes in the establishment of neighborhoods. This is clearly a case that shows the potential value of planners and designers stepping back and taking a more enabling, rather than prescriptive, approach to planning. In order to avoid the kind of mistakes that might have been made, such planners and designers should ask three basic questions in order to provide enabling systems that promote smart planning to shape an economically healthy future. First, what are the qualities or set of conditions that make this place unique? Second, what interventions are needed to make planning happen faster so that the population and tax base are stabilized? Third, what aspects of design need to be addressed in order to create a more inclusive and responsive environment that is, ultimately, a local and regional destination?

Enabling systems in planning and design policy need to reflect the linkages that exist between immigration and the physical environment in the following three areas: population growth, social networks, and adaptive neighborhood structure. The challenge here is to implement policies that capitalize on current demographic and economic trends while ensuring the creation of desirable and vibrant communities in the long term. Southwest Detroit is changing dramatically in terms of culture, ethnicity, and demand for urban amenities. These changes are signs of a much larger national transformation of the Latino cultural landscape. The changes along the West Vernor–Bagley Street Corridor can be seen in the economic, social, and cultural indications of the Latino community's presence.

Figure 17. Ethnic representation and vernacular art are present throughout the area's billboards and storefronts along the corridor. Photos by author.

COLUMBUS, OHIO: MORSE ROAD CORRIDOR AND SULLIVANT AVENUE

Context and Background

Unlike with the previous two case studies of Phoenix and Detroit, Columbus, Ohio, has not historically been a destination for Latino immigrants. Recent scholarship shows that the first Mexican and Tejano migrants arrived in Ohio following the end of World War I. Later, immigrants and refugees from other parts of Latin America found a home in Columbus and in other cities across Ohio. According to the Ohio Commission on Hispanic/Latino Affairs, in recent years Columbus has drawn a substantial number of Latino immigrants seeking construction and service jobs. As in other cities across America, most of these Latino immigrants are going to places where they think they can find employment or established communities of their compatriots. The Latino presence is becoming visible in two distinct areas of Columbus. The west side has been a magnet for largely Mexican immigrants principally along the Sullivant Avenue Corridor, slowly spreading from there. The other area that is becoming a favored destination of immigrants is the northeast part of Columbus along the Morse Road Corridor. This area is heavily populated by not only Latinos but by immigrants from Africa and Southeast Asia. Here, too, the principal Latino group is Mexicans.

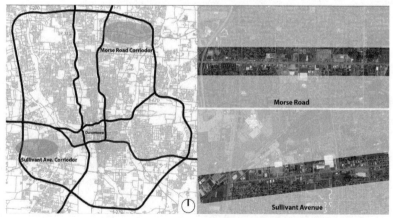

Figure 18. Latino corridors in Columbus, Ohio, can be found in two distinct areas: (1) the Morse Road Corridor in the northeast, and (2) Sullivant Avenue on the west side. Image by author.

The city's Latino community overall is growing at one of the fastest rates in the country, having doubled in the past ten years. Columbus currently ranks twenty-third among U.S. cities in Latino population.

A first glance at either Sullivant Avenue or Morse Road suggests a Latino barrio or "international corridor," as signs in Spanish and other foreign languages catch the eye. A closer inspection, however, especially in the Morse Corridor, reveals many white and African American entrepreneurs operating side by side with those of "newer" ethnicity. Most Latino immigrants, who have been arriving in large numbers since the 1990s, have not settled in distinct neighborhoods or ethnic enclaves. Instead, they can be found wherever rents are affordable, mostly in older post–World War II era suburbs, near strip malls, and in commercial corridors, as is the case with the Sullivant Avenue and Morse Road Corridors. The new trend among Latino immigrants, as well as with other ethnic groups, is for newcomers and the native born to intermingle without acknowledging any ethnic boundaries, in the manner of a suburban "salad bowl." This metaphor was first coined in 1959 by historian Carl Degler, who sought a better image for cultural change than the older term of "melting pot" (Degler 1984). Most scholars now agree with Degler that immigrants' cultural distinctiveness seldom melts completely away but rather contributes flavorful, fresh components to American society. The residential intermingling now happening in suburbia takes the salad bowl metaphor to a new level in many cities across the country, Columbus being a good example.

Analysis of the Local Conditions and the Presence of Threshold Elements

Sullivant Avenue
1. *Density:* The corridor is located seven miles west of downtown Columbus in a suburban neighborhood. The low population density of the area (2,425 people per square mile) does not meet the ideal minimum density (5,000 people per square mile) necessary to support convenience markets surrounding a targeted corridor. The corridor is considered a neighborhood subcenter characterized by convenience stores, ethnic supermarkets, and ethnic restaurants.

2. *Accessibility:* The area is accessible by car and public transportation. West Broad Street, which is located within the study area and runs parallel to Sullivant Avenue, is a U.S. national highway and a major east-west artery in Columbus. The corridor is also adjacent to the outer belt of the I-670 freeway.

3. *Safety:* The perception of safety in the area is low, possibly attributable to the sporadic nature of business activity and the large scale of buildings in the area. Most of the commercial areas lack sidewalks, discouraging pedestrian activity and increasing dependency on automobiles to navigate the site.

4. *Existing Retail:* The corridor has a low concentration of retail space. The largest Latino-owned business is Plaza Tapatia, one of the two largest Latino supermarkets in Columbus. This area is considered a new emergent destination for recent immigrants, most of whose businesses have been there only a few years. However, the area is growing rapidly, with new and different businesses forming. It is becoming a popular destination for Latino immigrants because of the products and services provided by the large ethnic supermarket.

5. *Capacity Building:* The presence and support of Latino representatives of nonprofit organizations is limited, and in many case residents are not aware of what types of services are available. As both Columbus and central Ohio in general are relatively new destinations for immigrants, the development of effective leadership and support for such immigrants is only in its formative stages. Various organizations offer some services and support with respect to employment (Defense Supply Center Columbus, DSCC), governmental assistance and cultural opportunities (Ohio Commission on Hispanic/Latino Affairs, OCHLA), immigration and health issues (Community Refugee and Immigration Services, CRIS), and small-business assistance (Hispanic Chamber of Commerce and Ohio Latino Small Business Development Center, SBDC).

Morse Street

1. *Density:* The corridor is located about eight miles north of downtown Columbus in a suburban neighborhood. The corridor is considered a neighborhood subcenter characterized by

convenience stores, ethnic supermarkets and restaurants, and a community center. There are also small department stores, as well as discount and home improvement stores. The area's population density of 5,145 people per square mile meets the ideal minimum density (5,000 people per square mile) to support convenience markets surrounding a targeted corridor.

2. *Accessibility:* The corridor is easily accessible by car and public transportation. Morse Road is a major transportation artery in Columbus, with direct access to I-75 and I-275 (the city's outer freeway belt).

3. *Safety:* The perception of safety in the area is very low, perhaps attributable to the transitory nature of the corridor. A lack of infrastructure and street amenities discourages pedestrian activity. Most of the businesses are accessed principally by automobile because of relatively long distances between the commercial establishments and residential areas.

4. *Existing Retail:* The corridor has a high concentration of retail and grocery businesses, the most noteworthy of which is La Michoacana Market, the largest Latino supermarket in Columbus. This area is considered a new emergent destination for recent immigrants from Latin America, Southeast Asia, and Somalia. The majority of its businesses have been in operation for only a few years. Rapid growth, however, is leading to the establishment of new and different businesses, and the corridor is becoming a popular destination for residents across the metropolitan area because of the unique products and services provided by the ethnic supermarkets, as well the distinctive ethnic dining experiences offered by local restaurants.

5. *Capacity Building:* See the "capacity building" section on Sullivan Avenue.

Demographic Trends and Impacts

The immigrant population in the state of Ohio has increased in the last twenty years, an increase that is reflected at the state, county, and city levels. Latino immigrants in Ohio account for large and growing shares of the economy, population, and electorate. In 2014 Latinos represented an estimated 3.4 percent of Ohio's population, up from about 3.1 percent in 2010 (Immigration Policy Center 2013).

Figure 19. Examples of adaptive uses along the Sullivant Avenue Corridor in Columbus, Ohio, include the adaptations of former shopping malls and strip malls. Photos by author.

According to the U.S. Census Bureau, Ohio gained an estimated 32,263 Latino residents between 2010 and 2014. That's an increase of about 9 percent. According to the Selig Center for Economic Growth at the University of Georgia, the 2014 purchasing power of Ohio's Latinos totaled $8.8 billion—an increase of 470 percent since 1990. In addition, the state's 9,722 Latino-owned businesses had sales and receipts of $2.3 billion and employed 11,562 people in 2007, according to the U.S. Census Bureau's Survey of Business Owners (Immigration Policy Center 2013). More than half of the Latinos live in four counties: Cuyahoga, Franklin, Lucas, and Lorain, home to some of the state's major urban centers. In electoral power, Latinos constituted 1.3 percent (or 74,000) of Ohio voters in the 2008 presidential elections, also according to the U.S. Census Bureau.

In 2011 Ohio's Latino community comprised 362,000 people, accounting for 3 percent of the state's total population. The median age was twenty-five years. Median annual personal earnings for those sixteen years and older was $20,000, compared to $29,400 for comparable non-Latino whites. According to the 2006 American Community Survey by the U.S. Census Bureau, Ohio's Latino population has grown 22.4 percent since 2000 and more than doubled since 1980. At the county level, the share of Franklin County's foreign-born population increased from 3.4 percent in 1990 to 6.0 percent in 2000 and to 9.0 percent (or 105,536 people) in 2011, according to the U.S. Census Bureau.

Columbus's Latino population has almost doubled since 2000. According to a report of the Brookings Institution (Frey 2001), between 2000 and 2008 the Columbus metropolitan area had the ninth highest rate of growth in Latino population among the hundred largest metropolitan areas in the United States. Also, according to William H. Frey, who is one of the study's authors and a Brookings demographer specializing in urban populations and immigration, what makes Columbus more attractive to immigrants over other cities in the state such as Cleveland or Cincinnati is the presence of Ohio State University and businesses that attract high- and low-skilled workers.

In terms of actual numbers, in 2010 the total population of Columbus was 787,033. Its Latino population was 44,359 (versus 17,527 in 2000), or 5.63 percent of its total population (versus 2.46 percent in 2000). The numbers represent an increase of 153 percent (or 26,832 residents) between 2000 and 2010.

Economic Trends and Impacts

The gains in population described in the previous section are also reflected in the economic impact that Latinos and other immigrant groups have made in the state of Ohio. At last count, businesses owned by Latinos and Asians had sales and receipts of $9.1 billion and

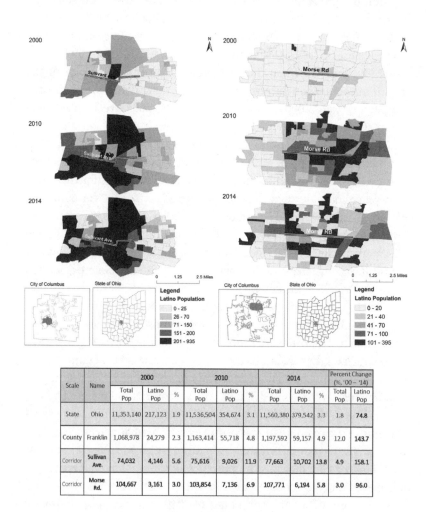

Scale	Name	2000			2010			2014			Percent Change (%, '00 – '14)	
		Total Pop	Latino Pop	%	Total Pop	Latino Pop	%	Total Pop	Latino Pop	%	Total Pop	Latino Pop
State	Ohio	11,353,140	217,123	1.9	11,536,504	354,674	3.1	11,560,380	379,542	3.3	1.8	74.8
County	Franklin	1,068,978	24,279	2.3	1,163,414	55,718	4.8	1,197,592	59,157	4.9	12.0	143.7
Corridor	Sullivan Ave.	74,032	4,146	5.6	75,616	9,026	11.9	77,663	10,702	13.8	4.9	158.1
Corridor	Morse Rd.	104,667	3,161	3.0	103,854	7,136	6.9	107,771	6,194	5.8	3.0	96.0

Note) *For Data Source and Boundary Selection, Refer to Appendix.

Figure 20. Latino population change within Latino corridors in Columbus, Ohio. The Latino population of Columbus is largely concentrated in two distinct areas: (1) the Morse Road Corridor in the northeast, and (2) Sullivant Avenue on the west side. Image by author.

employed more than 63,000 people. Ohio is also home to the nation's second-largest Somali population, whose many businesses contribute to the state's economy. At a time when the economy is still recovering, Ohio cannot afford to alienate such important components of its labor force, tax base, and business community (Immigration Policy Center 2013). The 2012 purchasing power of Ohio's Latinos totaled $8.2 billion—an increase of 432 percent since 1990. Between 2010 and 2013 alone, Latino buying power in Ohio increased from $6,897,242 to $8,418,188 (a 22.1 percent increase), according to the Selig Center for Economic Growth at the University of Georgia (Humphreys 2013), and Ohio ranks twenty-first in the country in Latino buying power. This increased buying power among immigrants is reflected in the number of ethnic entrepreneurships that have formed along the Morse Road and Sullivant Avenue Corridors.

The case of Columbus's ethnic entrepreneurs is somewhat unusual. Most immigrant Latino, Somali, and Southeast Asian groups have settled in areas that were very successful commercial cores in the 1970s and 1980s. For instance, Morse Road in the northeast part of the city was the home of Northland Mall, which closed in 2002 as the formerly prosperous neighborhood began to decline. However, in recent years immigrant entrepreneurs have opened stores and restaurants in vacant and abandoned commercial buildings there. This phenomenon started an economic and cultural revitalization in the area. The Morse Road Corridor and the Sullivant Avenue Corridor are located in strategic locations now poised for future growth. Easy access to interstate highways provides excellent connectivity to the rest of the city. Redevelopment of both the Northland Mall site on Morse Road and the Westland Mall site on Sullivant Avenue represent exciting opportunities for commercial redevelopment.

Today, banners in Spanish and Somali along Morse Road advertise vacancies in apartment communities. A quick look at people walking on the streets, biking, using public transportation, and relaxing on the porches shows that the once declining neighborhood is coming back to life. Because of the density of apartments and small houses, public transportation functions well here. Morse Road is one of the city's busiest mass transit routes and is well connected to other parts of the metropolitan region, an important feature that attracts even more immigrants.

Figure 21. Examples of adaptive uses along the Morse Road Corridor in Columbus, Ohio. Photos by author.

One of the key findings regarding the Morse Road and Sullivant Avenue Corridors is that an affordable and diverse housing stock can provide options in the area for a mix of incomes and household types. Most residential areas are in close proximity to jobs and services (Kinninger and Martin 2014). Morse Road contains 319 retail establishments and government facilities. The top four industries in this area are auto-related businesses, eating and drinking establishments, miscellaneous retail, and apparel/accessory stores. The business density is extremely high relative to the corridor's length: 86.21 businesses per square mile. In comparison, according to the Martin Prosperity Institute, the New York City metro area's business density is calculated at 79 businesses per square mile. The businesses are important because of the jobs that they create. The businesses along the corridor operate on both a local and regional scale through automotive and retail establishments. The advantage of the density and the diversity of services is that they help pull people from a larger area, creating a destination point.

Table 3. Columbus, Ohio, Morse Road Corridor ranking of businesses in the area based on quantity and type during the interview and inventory process.

Ranking	Type of business	Number of businesses by type	Representative businesses
1	Ethnic markets (mercados latinos)	21	Makola-Market, Three C Foodmart, Romanos, Five Star Auto, Stop and Go Groceries, Buckeye Market, Halal Meats, Barako Food Mart, Aaron Discount Center, La Mega Michoacana, Ameristop Food Mart, Shangrila Corner Store, Berekum African Market
2	Ethnic food	20	Huong Vietnamese Restaurant, Momo Ghar, Namaste Indo-Nepali Cuisine, Dabakh Restaurant, China Buffer, Golden Phoenix, Taqueria Jalisco, Minerva Market, Layla Kitchen, Xochimilco Taqueria, African Paradise, Panaderia Mi Pueblo, Dakshin at Morse

continued

Table 3. *continued*

Ranking	Type of business	Number of businesses by type	Representative businesses
3	Social services and nonprofit organizations	13	Bhutanese Nepali Community of Columbus, Gillie Senior Recreation Center, Northland Church of Christ Child Care, Igleisa de Cristo, Vineyard Columbus Northside Food Pantry, Calvary Presbyterian Church, Goodwill, New Mt. Sinai Church of God in Christ, Global Medical Center, Ascension Lutheran Church, Columbus Human Arts and Technology Academy
4	Auto-related business (used car sales)	12	Mr. Tire Auto Service Center, Miracle Motor Mart, King Used Tires, BP Auto Sales, Pablo's New and Used Tires, Enterprise Car Sale, DriveTime Used Cars, Tom Auto Upholstery, Columbus Motor Car, Discount Auto Repair, Royal Five Auto Sales, Life Affordable Auto Sales
5	Personal services (beauty shops, barbershops, natural medicine)	8	African Euphoria Braiding, Hair Plus, Nail Tech, Nada African Hair Braiding, Another Level Beauty Salon, Estetica Angelica, Tame Hair Studio
7	Miscellaneous	8	Pawn Into Cash, Credit Union, Suarez Tax and Documents Prep, Accu Cash Pawn Shop, Lev's Pawn Shop, E-Z Cash Pawn Shop, Global Money Transfer, Cash in a Dash Pawn Shop
8	Specialty products and services	7	Payless Shoe Source, Wireless World, Dollar Store, Dollar General, It's All One Dollar, Global Mall, Dollar Tree
9	Special-occasion shops	4	Fashion City, Angie's Bridal and Tuxedo, Julian Wireless, Surplus World Inc.
10	Entertainment (bars, nightclubs)	3	8 Ball Sports Bar and Billiards, Rosie O'Grady's, Ginevra Café

Note: Restaurants and stores along the Morse Road are beginning to more closely resemble the immigrant populations that have moved into the area in the past decade, including Somali, West African, and Latino. In general, businesses in the area tend to be patronized by all the different immigrant groups present in the area.

Table 4. Columbus, Ohio, Sullivant Avenue Corridor ranking of businesses in the area based on quantity and type during the interview and inventory process.

Ranking	Type of business	Number of businesses by type	Representative businesses
1	Ethnic food	21	Panaderia Oaxaqueña, El Nopalito, Mezcal Los Rios, Los Galapagos, Mariscos San Blas, La Plaza Tapatia, Taqueria Delicias Mexican Grill, Decan Dabar/Khyber, Emelio's, Taqueria San Angel, Los Chilangos Taco Truck, Bakery El Rico Pan, Minellis, Zacatecas, Koki's Tortillas
2	Ethnic markets (mercados latinos)	15	Day's Drive In, Corner Drive Thru, Ayan Grocery Store, La Michoacana Market, Luc's Asian Market Groceries, My Deah's Store, La Bodega Supermarket, Alex Market, Speedy Mart
3	Auto-related business	14	Scott and Son Concrete Trucking, Quick Auto Sales, Service King Collison Repair, Tire Zone, Ortega Auto Repair, Banadir Auto Sales, Autosol Car Dealer, Jack's Tires, C&T Auto Sales
4	Specialty products and services	7	Lincoln Park Laundromat, Family Dollar, Dollar General, Super Look
5	Entertainment (bars, nightclubs)	6	El MusicOn Latino, Shaker's Bar and Grill, Nico's Pub and Patio, Jay's Sports Lounge
6	Social services and nonprofit organizations	5	World Mission Church of God, Ohio Hispanic Coalition, La Voz Hispana Newspaper
7	Special-occasion shops	4	Payless Shoe Source, Islamic Bookstore
8	Miscellaneous	4	Western Union, Money Gram

The once dilapidated and abandoned small strip shopping centers and "big box" retail outlets, which are easily reached by foot from nearby apartment complexes and accessible to immigrants who depend on public transportation, have flowered into vibrant miniature "downtowns." Most cater to several ethnic groups. Latino *tiendas* (grocery stores) and Somali markets offer a mix of basic American and imported goods. As populations grow, restaurants and specialty stores do with them. Based on a food network map generated in the study, restaurants and groceries are largely concentrated in two locations. The first is the intersection of Cleveland Avenue and Morse Road; the second is the intersection of East Dublin–Granville Road and Cleveland Avenue. There are twenty-eight ethnic restaurants, nine groceries, and six food trucks along the Morse Corridor. The most prevalent cuisines offered are Chinese, Japanese, Mexican, Somali, and Vietnamese. The abundance of culture in the Morse Road Corridor provides the residents of Northland, and of Columbus as a whole, an opportunity to experience multiple cultures within a manageable traveling distance.

The social infrastructure of the corridors is composed of schools, churches, community centers, and public services. Schools are fundamental in every community because they provide education to the youngest generation, the future of each community. Public services are made up of government agencies, which provide important protection, stability, and assistance to residents. Community centers include actual community centers, recreational centers, libraries, and food pantries. These locations provide spaces where residents can connect and the overall health and wellness of a community can be maintained. However, awareness of the nature and availability of these services by local residents and small-business owners is not without problems. Many local entrepreneurs acknowledge that they feel lost when dealing with government bureaucracy. They scratch their heads over the ten-year, $1.2 million tax abatement that Eau Claire, Wisconsin-based Menard Inc. landed, and remain at a loss about how to seek similar concessions for their own *local* businesses (Ghose 2010).

Summary and Implications for Future Planning

The Morse Road Corridor was the site of a service learning community design studio taught by the author in the spring of 2014 as part of the City and Regional Planning program at Ohio State University in Columbus. Some of the data, outreach and engagement, findings, and recommendations were carried out by a group of ten students under the author's guidance. Parts of the collected data, analysis, and findings are presented here. The research and design process was divided into four different phases. In phase one the focus was on qualitative data analysis and mapping accomplished through a hands-on

Figure 22. Multiethnic shopping plazas are now commonplace along Morse Road and Sullivant Avenue. Here, entrepreneurs from Mexico, El Salvador, Lebanon, and Somalia share public infrastructure. Photos by author.

approach by the students. The tools and techniques applied in this phase included site visits, photo documentation, visual assessment, and informal and unstructured interviews with resident stakeholders. Phase two was about quantitative research performed by the students. Sources included census data, demographics, and economic trends in the region and in the specific study area, as well as secondary sources such as market analyses and demographic reports from both public and private sources. Phase three was about community outreach and engagement. Through these activities the team sought to engage community members of all ages with meaningful opportunities to provide input to the process of developing a vision for their community. The process of inclusion and engaging communities in decision making is as important as the outcomes (Cohen et al. 2009). In phase four, all the data analysis and outcomes from outreach activities were compiled and synthesized to help inform recommendations for future development in the area, with the focus on the immigrant communities that live, work, and play there.

The Morse Road commercial corridor, site of the former Northland Mall, and Sullivant Avenue, site of the former Westland Mall, are the only two places in Columbus where one can get a temporary henna tattoo and then cross the street for a piñata, fresh fruit and vegetables, fresh-baked bread, pastries, and tortillas. The immigrant-owned businesses along Morse Road and Sullivant Avenue are credited with preventing the widespread vacancies that were feared when the malls closed in 2002. According to neighborhood groups, ethnic stores sprinkled amid national discount chains have created a diverse destination that is attracting traffic and therefore more businesses.

The immigrant community is going to play a big part in future Columbus development, generating new types of businesses and customers. Immigrants are part of a social, cultural, and economic revitalization that includes businesses that did not flee the Morse and Sullivant Corridors and new charter schools that occupy once vacant retail space. Immigrants are reshaping these ethnic commercial corridors into a destination—not just a neighborhood convenience district, but a cultural destination that can provide social networks for new immigrants. The business activity in the area is brisk. Since 2002, the Franklin County auditor's office has issued about 180 new vendor permits in the mile-long stretch of Morse Road between the mall site at Karl Road and Cleveland Avenue. The list is heavily dominated by African names, with a Somali pool hall and African restaurants and markets selling meat that is halal, that is, butchered according to Islamic law (Ghose 2010).

The current era of change has been most remarkable for Columbus. The landscape has begun to shift dramatically from once abandoned strip malls to thriving commercial venues along the Morse and Sullivant suburban commercial corridors. A key characteristic of these new types of immigrant communities are the "salad bowl" suburbs they have fostered. But the question here is whether Columbus will eventually itself become a salad-bowl suburb, or if the experiences of integration between new immigrants and longtime residents in the corridors is just an illusion. Both the northeast and the west sides of Columbus are currently struggling with inadequate resources for schools and perceptions of high rates of crime, as well as with other social and cultural challenges.

INDIANAPOLIS, INDIANA: WEST WASHINGTON STREET

Context and Background

Latinos have been a presence in Indianapolis for the past thirty years. The recent influx can be attributed to an established base of Latinos who have been living in Indianapolis for five to ten years and who have attracted relatives after they decided to immigrate to the United States. This process is known as chain migration. Indianapolis can be considered a new gateway for immigrants because of the relatively recent presence of Latinos in the area. Unlike in other traditional Latino gateway destinations, where Latino presence dates back further into the twentieth century, in Indianapolis Latinos have bypassed central city neighborhoods and settled down in various parts of the city. Latinos have moved into older "middle-ring" suburbs in the west, east, and southeast of the city. The area selected for this case study is a four-mile section along West Washington Street between the White River just west of downtown and the I-465 interstate, an area characterized by mid- to low-density land use. Its character, in terms of modern development practices, is neither urban nor suburban; rather, it is an unplanned mixture of population densities and land uses. The area along this corridor has two very distinct

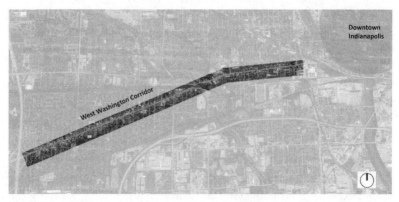

Figure 23. West Washington Corridor context in Indianapolis, Indiana. Image by author.

sections: one from White River Parkway to South Tibbs Avenue and a second from South Holt Road to South Mickley Avenue. In the late 1890s parts of this area were initially populated by German, Irish, and Slovenian immigrants. Historically, this area has been home to many immigrant groups. In 1900 the U.S. Census Bureau reported sixteen different nationalities living in the area, including Hungarians, Poles, Austrians, and Macedonians (Sports 1998). Since the 1990s the area has been the focus of large, federally funded revitalization programs.

Washington Street was part of what was called the "National Road," which developed in the 1840s. It later became U.S. 40 as a part of the National Highway System. This area was the "Main Street" of Indianapolis, as it carried thousands of pioneers westward to new territories (Arnold and Turrin 2012). This transcontinental traffic stimulated the development of commercial activity in the city's downtown and in adjacent areas of Washington Street. With the introduction of the interstate in the 1950s, the importance of Washington Street diminished. Today, the role and identity of Washington Street remain significant at the local level, as it is a primary transportation arterial to employment centers and neighborhoods, and provides direct accessibility to rail, bus, and air transportation (Arnold and Turrin 2012). Visual inventory and analysis of the area reveals the challenges it faces, including lack of parking, visual disorder, perception as an unsafe public sphere, and high building rehabilitation costs, all making it difficult to compete with other commercial areas around the city.

Analysis of the Local Conditions and the Presence of Threshold Elements in the West Washington Street Corridor

1. *Density*: The corridor stretches from downtown Indianapolis to a low-density suburban neighborhood 5.5 miles to the west of it. The corridor is considered a neighborhood subcenter due to the limited number of small businesses, convenience stores, and grocery outlets. On the other hand, a large number of used-car dealerships are present. The density in the area is 3,499 people per square mile, which does not meet the ideal minimum density (5,000 people per square mile) necessary to support convenience markets surrounding a targeted corridor.

2. *Accessibility*: The area features both easy access to highway transportation as well as the availability of public transportation. The corridor is a national highway and is connected to the outer belt of I-74 in the western part of the metropolitan area.

3. *Safety*: The perception of safety in the area is mixed, perhaps due to the high level of traffic and a lack of sidewalks and street amenities along some parts of the corridor, which tends to discourage pedestrian activity.

4. *Existing Retail*: The corridor has been growing in recent years, with a mix of businesses that reflect its changing demographics.

5. *Capacity Building*: Although Indianapolis is considered a new gateway for recent immigrants, support for the immigrant community from nonprofit organizations has been strong and well organized. Organizations offering such support include the Indiana Latino Institute, La Plaza, the Hispanic-Latino Minority Health Coalition of Greater Indianapolis, the Indiana Latino Coalition Against Domestic and Sexual Violence, and El Centro Comunal Latino (CCL).

Demographic Trends and Impact

According to U.S. Census estimates, in 2015 there were approximately 426,000 Latinos in the entire state of Indiana, or 0.8 percent of all Latinos in the United States. In Marion County, whose seat is Indianapolis, 77,352 Latinos constitute approximately 9.4 percent of the county's 820,445 residents. The Latino population in Indiana is relatively small. However, this has been changing rapidly over the past ten years as Latinos have developed into the fastest-growing

Figure 24. Successful examples of adaptive uses in mixed-use development. Photos by author.

population group in many counties across the state. In 2011 the U.S. Census Bureau reported a 55 percent increase (from 214,536 to 389,707) in Indiana's Latino population over the previous decade. These numbers do not include an estimated 3 to 5 percent of the population who likely went uncounted because they refused to provide information (Rogers and Strange 2015). The population increase was even more pronounced in the Indianapolis area encompassing Marion County, which more than doubled its Latino population, from about 33,000 to more than 84,000. Currently, the state's population is 84 percent white, approximately 9 percent black, and 6 percent Latino, with the remaining 1 percent made up of other minorities (Rogers and Strange 2015). Experts predict that in the next decade Latinos could surpass in size the state's black population, which stands at roughly 591,000. According to the Indiana Business Research Center of the Indiana University Kelley School of Business (Conover, Rogers, and Kinghorn 2005), the growth of the Latino population is due principally to immigration and people obtaining legal permanent residence in the state. Also, as discussed in a previous chapter, the Latino population tends to be younger, with higher fertility rates that are contributing to the rise. The median age for Latinos in Indiana is twenty-four, compared to thirty-seven for the overall state population. In addition, there are larger numbers of children in the overall minority population compared to the white population. According to the U.S. Census Bureau, the non-Latino white population of children under eighteen has dropped by 96,000, while the minority population of children increased by more than 129,000 in the past decade. The Latino population is projected to add 284,600 residents to the state by 2030. This figure equates to a 100 percent increase over the 2005 figures and will account for 38 percent of the state's total growth (Kinghorn 2008). As a share of Indiana's total population, the number of Latinos is expected to jump from 4.5 percent to 8 percent by 2030. Nearly all counties will see relatively substantial increases in their Latino populations. Counties expected to have the largest numeric increases are Marion (87,800), Elkhart (33,500), and Lake (23,300) (Kinghorn 2008).

In the state's capital the Latino population growth has been more dramatic. For instance, between 2000 and 2013 the Latino population of Indianapolis increased by 195.5 percent (Rogers and Strange 2015).

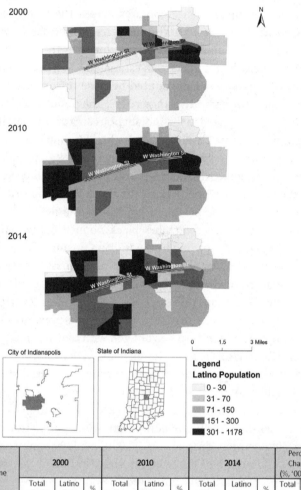

Scale	Name	2000			2010			2014			Percent Change (%, '00 – '14)	
		Total Pop	Latino Pop	%	Total Pop	Latino Pop	%	Total Pop	Latino Pop	%	Total Pop	Latino Pop
State	Indiana	6,080,485	214,536	3.5	6,483,802	389,707	6.0	6,542,411	411,536	6.3	7.6	**91.8**
County	Marion	860,454	33,290	3.9	903,393	84,466	9.3	919,336	88,171	9.6	6.8	**164.9**
Corridor	West Washington St.	60,778	3,582	5.9	59,271	10,968	18.5	59,021	11,642	19.7	-2.9	**225.0**

Note) *For Data Source and Boundary Selection, Refer to Appendix.

Figure 25. Latino population change in the West Washington Corridor. Image by author.

According to the U.S. Census Bureau, 9.4 percent of the population in Indianapolis is Latino, versus only 6 percent for the state as a whole. A large part of this Latino population is of Mexican origin. As a response to this accelerated growth in central Indiana, leaders have been taking steps to better understand the culture and needs of this ethnic group. For instance, over the years Indianapolis police have hired translators for each of its districts to aid and facilitate communication between officers and Latino residents. The number of services available to Latinos in central Indiana has also increased substantially over the years, ranging from the fields of health and education to advocacy and research. A large effort has been undertaken to ensure that families know about these resources through a new umbrella organization, the Latino American Outreach Association Inc.

Economic Trends and Impacts

The economic impacts that Latino immigrants have on the city of Indianapolis and across the state are reflected in many areas, including businesses, housing, and tax contributions. According to the Selig Center for Economic Growth at the University of Georgia, the 2014 purchasing power of Latinos in Indiana totaled $8.5 billion—an increase of 717 percent since 1990 (Humphreys 2014). The state's 8,558 Latino-owned businesses had sales and receipts of $1.7 billion and employed 14,304 people in 2007, according to the U.S. Census Bureau's Survey of Business Owners (American Immigration Council 2015). In addition, research has shown that Latino immigration boosts housing values in communities. For instance, between 2000 and 2010, according to the Americas Society/Council of the Americas, the value added by immigration to the price of an average home in Marion County was $3,635.

In terms of tax contributions, Latinos in Indiana paid a total of $938 million in federal taxes and $514 million in state and local taxes in 2013, according to the Partnership for a New American Economy. Of this, foreign-born Latinos paid $473.7 million in federal taxes and $251.4 million in state and local taxes in 2013. The federal tax contribution of Indiana's Latino population included $677.5 million to Social Security and $158 million to Medicare in 2013, and, of this, foreign-born Latinos contributed $341 million to Social Security and $79.8 million to Medicare (ITEP 2013). It is also important to take into account the economic contributions of unauthorized immigrants in the state. Unauthorized immigrants in Indiana paid $108.9 million in state and local taxes in 2010, including $74.4 million in sales taxes, $25.4 million in state income taxes, and $9 million in property taxes, according to data from the Institute for Taxation and Economic Policy (ITEP 2013). It is estimated that if unauthorized immigrants in Indiana had legal status, they would annually pay $141.7 million in state and local taxes, including $78.8 million in sales taxes, $53.3 million in state income taxes, and $9.6 million in property taxes (American Immigration Council 2015). In other words, failure to provide these immigrants with legal status costs Indiana at least $40 million annually.

Indianapolis has proven a welcoming environment for entrepreneurs. A study published in 2014 of Latino buying power and entrepreneurship ranked Indianapolis over other major cities such as Chicago, Philadelphia, and Jersey City, New Jersey, in terms of business friendliness. The Indiana capital was ranked just below New York City. The rankings were based on data from the U.S. Census Bureau, the Council for Community and Economic Research, the U.S. Bureau of Labor Statistics, the Federal Deposit Insurance Corporation, and the Tax Foundation (Bernardo 2014). In addition, Indianapolis's local government has made efforts to support and promote minority-owned businesses. The city's long-standing policy of allocating 20 percent of municipal contracts to firms owned by women and minorities was increased in 2014 by Mayor Greg Ballard to 33 percent, doubling the number of Hispanic businesses affected (Akoukou 2015).

Latino-owned and operated businesses are significant contributors to Indianapolis's local economy. According to the Hispanic Business Council, the impact of Latino-owned business sales taxes is about $230 million annually, and the entire Latino community has an impact of $400 million dollars. These numbers do not include public safety taxes, school taxes, income taxes, or other taxes. When all taxes and assessments are considered, the total economic impact statewide comes to 7 billion dollars, a 40 percent increase in five years (Akoukou 2015).

Summary and Implications for Future Planning

Most of the data and information for this case study was collected during site visits and windshield surveys that helped assess the spatial

Table 5. Indianapolis, Indiana, West Washington Street Corridor ranking of businesses in the area based on quantity and type during the interview and inventory process.

Ranking	Type of business	Number of businesses by type	Representative businesses
1	Used auto and auto-related businesses	28	J R's Used Tires, 4 Friends Auto Sales, Reyes Body Shop, El Mata Auto Repair, Auto Trust International, Cibao Motors, Joe's Auto Sales, Philip's Auto Sales, Starter Alternator, Topcat Motors, A-1 Auto & Truck Inc., Dependable Auto Sales, Indiana Quality Used Tires, Auto Mex, Kokoo Auto Sales, Shorty's Taller Mecanico, Alex Auto Sales, Curtis Motor Sales, Autos La Piedad, Rodriguez Mechanics and Alignment, Big R Auto Sales, Borimex Auto Sales, Payless Car Rental
2	Ethnic food	16	Mama Ines Mexican Bakery, Pollo Michoacano, Birrieria Andrade, Taqueria Mi Costa, La Salsita, El Volken Mexican, Kokos Locos, Taqueria El Ranchito, La Fogata Mexicana, El Paisa, Somali Cuisine, Major
3	Ethnic markets (mercados latinos)	14	Carniceria Puebla, Family Dollar, El Encanto de Yemeya, Carniceria El Ranchito, Hana Market, Dollar Tree, Honduras Express, Antojitos Puebla, African Market, Halal Market
4	Personal services (beauty shops, barbershops, natural medicine)	9	Los Nitidos Barber Shop, Regalos y Decoraciones Erika, Evelyn Beauty Salon, Botanica San Lazaro, Taxes y Servicios Marina, Nice Nails
5	Social services and nonprofit organizations	7	Iglesia Cristiana Westside, Vida Nueva United Methodist, Iglesisa De Dios Pentecostal, Apostolic Life Church, Goodwill Store
6	Specialty products and services	6	Electro Hogar, Maria's Travel Services, Casa Mateo, Liquorland
7	Entertainment (bars, nightclubs)	5	Bulseye Lounge, Studio 51
8	Miscellaneous	4	Western Union, First Cash Pawn

and visual aspects of the Latino landscape and identified key elements of the urban pattern present in the area, such as street activities, building façades, colors, murals, fences, and store frontages. In addition, the site visits were supplemented by informal interviews with key leaders, stakeholders, and representatives of nonprofit organizations that work with Latinos in the area. The many institutions in the area include La Plaza, whose mission is to strengthen central Indiana by advocating and preparing Latino students for educational success and connecting Latino families to health and social welfare services; the Indiana Latino Institute, whose mission is to improve health and advance education for the Indiana Latino community through statewide advocacy, research, and culturally responsive programs; and the Local Initiatives Support Corporation (LISC) of Indianapolis, which is the local office of the country's largest community development corporation. LISC is dedicated to transforming distressed neighborhoods into healthy and sustainable communities—good places to work, do business, and raise children. LISC has had an impact in many areas across the city where Latino immigrants live, work, and play. Some of these areas include the Northeast Corridor, the near west, and the northwest. Over the past twenty years, LISC Indianapolis has invested $202 million and leveraged additional investments of more than $727 million for programs and projects across Indianapolis.

A visual survey of businesses in the area reveals that the West Washington Corridor is home to a large and diverse fabric of existing businesses. In addition to being stakeholders, these businesses are also the guardians of the public realm (Arnold and Turrin 2012). To better understand the dynamics of the corridor from White River Parkway to South Tibbs Avenue, a business inventory was conducted. There were a total of approximately sixty-eight ground-floor businesses. According to a business survey conducted by the city in 2012, businesses in the area met the following criteria: (1) the businesses had a positive impact on the surrounding community; (2) business sales and incomes were strongly correlated to a safe and accessible public environment; and (3) the businesses were dependent on daily retail sales and repeat clientele. The same business survey also revealed that 51 percent of businesses in the area are Latino owned. There is a significant presence of Latino business owners on West Washington Street that caters to the large Latino community in the adjacent neighborhoods. Informal interviews with owners of Latino businesses emphasized the strong identity that West Washington Street has as a Latino shopping destination. Most of the businesses

Figure 26. Examples of successful Latino businesses in Indianapolis. Photos by author.

in the area have operated for a median of six years. The majority of businesses under this median figure have been in operation only one to two years, while the majority of businesses over the median have been in operation over ten years. Established businesses have developed loyal clientele through unique products and quality service. Typically, business owners and managers live near or above their places of work.

Analyses and examinations of the Latino built environment along the West Washington Corridor have uncovered a pattern in language as to how residents use, imagine, and construct space. As Latinos have settled into cities, they have brought attitudes about housing, land, and public space that differ from how their houses and neighborhoods were originally planned, designed, and constructed (Rojas 1991). Some of the key elements of Latino urban pattern in the area include fences, front porches, front yards, murals, and store signs. One the most striking features of the area is the number of used-car dealerships and car repair-related businesses. In March 2016, when the visual inventory was taken, there were forty-one used car dealerships along the corridor. Most of these automobile-related businesses are located in the second half of the corridor that extends from South Holt Road to South Mickley Avenue. Analysis of Google aerial maps of the area shows that most of these businesses have opened in the last five to seven years.

West Washington business owners and residents stated that some the best qualities of the study area are both physically and community based. The best physical qualities identified included the corridor's strategic access to major employment, transportation, and cultural centers; use as a primary traffic route; and historic identity as part of the National Road. The best community qualities of West Washington included the existing concentration of small businesses, Hispanic community/cultural diversity, and neighborhood residents.

SUMMARY OF FINDINGS AND CONCLUSION
The commercial corridors presented in these case studies are in the process of becoming, or have become, local Main Streets with vibrant commercial centers that help maintain the social networks that provide residents with ties to their Latin American home countries while acclimating new immigrants and contributing to the creation of more

resilient communities. Researchers have argued that direct access to commercial establishments and public transit systems are some of the most important spatial amenities in Latino neighborhoods (Diaz and Torres 2012; Singer, Hardwick, and Brettel 2008). These qualities are present in all four study areas.

A shared element across the case studies is that the most common reason given for establishing businesses and residences in these areas was the presence of jobs, family, friends, and people with similar backgrounds—what is often referred to as "chain migration." Most immigrants arrived during the late 1990s to mid-2000s. Entrepreneurs also noted that these areas were attractive because property ownership was affordable and they had access to public transportation systems. Unlike the immigrants who arrived in the late nineteenth and mid-twentieth centuries, settling in distinct ethnic enclaves like Little Italy, Chinatown, or Greek Town, this new wave of immigrants scattered to where rents were affordable, mostly in older, post–World War II era suburbs (Hanchett 2010). It has been confirmed by research and scholars that Latino immigrants tend to scatter through neighborhoods where they are a small share of the population rather than clustering in ethnic enclaves (Smith and Furuseth 2006; Suro 2002). This has been the case with new gateway destinations such as Columbus and Indianapolis.

Ownership and rents in these commercial corridors have been affordable because of the high number of vacancies. At one time most of these commercial corridors had been economically successful, but they could not meet the demands presented by factors such as more automobile-oriented shopping patterns, larger retail space requirements, and the convenience of online shopping, all of which made it more difficult for traditional urban neighborhood commercial areas to compete in the regional commercial marketplace. Older urban commercial areas face the additional challenges presented by lack of parking, visual disorder, perception of lack of safety, high building rehabilitation costs, and dilapidated public infrastructure. At the same time these areas have become very attractive to new immigrants because of the affordable rents and property values. The opportunities presented by underutilized physical and social infrastructure can facilitate the entrepreneurial process for immigrants. In turn, the increasing number of ethnic businesses has reduced the number of vacant buildings and vacant lots.

The businesses in these four case studies have been able to reach out to three broad markets. First, and most accessible, is the neighborhood market. This market is oriented to meeting basic neighborhood needs. Examples of this type of business include general merchandise stores, convenience stores, pharmacies, grocery stores, fast-food services, bakeries, and beauty/barber shops. The second market is the regional market. This market consists of the unique products and services offered along the commercial corridors that are not generally found in regional cities and towns. The businesses in this category include specialized auto services, professional services, restaurants, and Latino products and services. The third market operates on a statewide scale. This market is the smallest of the three. However, unique products and services targeted toward the Latino community have attracted customers both by word-of-mouth and through bilingual advertising in statewide distributed magazines and newspapers.

During the informal interviews with entrepreneurs in all of the case studies, some barriers and challenges emerged. One of the key questions asked was: what were the biggest obstacles you faced in setting up a business here? The question was open-ended, with no preordained list of responses, yet the answers for the most part corresponded with those of other studies on this topic. For instance, the responses included lack of financing and access to start-up money, the lack of social and professional networks, lack of knowledge and understanding about local rules and regulations, lack of experience in marketing and developing clientele, dealing with bureaucracy, lack of a business plan, business expenses (taxes, rent, merchandise), lack of proficient language skills, lack of knowledge of where to go for help and available resources, and lack of knowledge on how to start and grow a business.

The demographic characteristics of self-employment among immigrants are reflected in age as well as in time spent in the United States. Those immigrants who have been in United States for more than ten years have a higher rate of self-employment than those who have been in the country for less than ten years. Much of this difference is correlated to an established immigrant's higher age. The informal interviews also revealed that many immigrants first work in wage employment before moving on to self-employment, with fewer being self-employed immediately after immigration.

There were common factors that attracted immigrants to their city of residency: their destination city was where family, a spouse, or friends already resided; the business environment; educational opportunities for their children; paid employment and wages waiting for them; and knowledge of a low cost of living characterized by affordable housing and businesses.

Summary of Key Findings Across Four Case Studies

This chapter has explored four case studies from diverse urban areas across the country and sought to understand the factors that contribute to the establishment of Latino neighborhoods in urban areas, and, in turn, how these communities contribute to the creation of social, economic, and cultural resilience for their residents. The focus was on ethnic entrepreneurship, which is one of the primary drivers of any local economy, as well as on some of the impacts in the social and cultural spheres. The economic benefits of entrepreneurship included the creation of new employment opportunities for local residents and promotion of greater regional economic development. Because immigrants overall are more entrepreneurial and have higher business formation rates than the native born, immigrant-owned businesses make sizable contributions to the U.S. economy nationally and locally. In the four cities examined—Phoenix, Detroit, Columbus, and Indianapolis— immigrant entrepreneurs have played an important role in the local community's commercial development. They have opened retail shops, restaurants, and markets, and they have started service businesses as CPAs and electricians. They fill in gaps within certain niches where particular goods and services are needed. Immigrant businesses have also been revitalizing streetscapes and neighborhoods—places within urban areas that may have been in decline and at risk of becoming areas of blight. Community leaders and entrepreneurs have been working hard to transform these areas into vibrant ethnic commercial corridors. Their efforts have been well received by residents and businesses alike, and have contributed to a reversal in fortunes for once derelict or moribund retail corridors. Strategies applied in these areas provide examples of adaptive reuse in which infrastructure is refreshed and the retail mix altered to complement neighborhood development. All the corridors

Table 6. Summary of takeaway points across four case studies.

Commercial corridor takeaway points

	McDowell Road, Phoenix, Arizona	West Vernor–Bagley, Detroit, Michigan	Morse Road, Columbus, Ohio	Sullivant Avenue, Columbus, Ohio	West Washington, Indianapolis, Indiana
Type (refers to trade area from which a corridor draws customers)	Neighborhood subcenter: with convenience store, grocery, pharmacy, dry cleaner, etc. Neighborhood center: supermarket, variety store, post office 8,085 people per sq. mile	Neighborhood center: supermarket, variety store, post office Specialty center: concentration of entertainment, restaurants, off-price goods, arts, or other 5,733 people per sq. mile	Neighborhood center: supermarket, variety store, post office Community center: discount department store, home improvement store 5,145 people per sq. miles	Neighborhood subcenter: with convenience store, grocery, pharmacy, dry cleaner, etc. 2,425 people per sq. mile	Neighborhood subcenter: with convenience store, grocery, pharmacy, dry cleaner, etc. Specialty center: concentration of used-car dealerships, off-price goods, or other. ,499 people per sq. mile
Context and character (refers to dominant physical and functional layout of the corridor)	Pedestrian/transit corridor: sidewalk-oriented, continuous streetwalls, separate property ownership, predominantly on-street parking	Pedestrian/transit corridor: sidewalk-oriented, continuous streetwalls, separate property ownership, predominantly on-street parking	Auto-oriented strip: piecemeal development and ownership, setbacks, free off-street parking, frequent curb cuts	Mixed character: strongly exhibits two or more characteristics (auto-oriented strip and transit corridor)	Mixed character: strongly exhibits two or more characteristics (auto-oriented strip and transit corridor)

	Redeveloping with good mix	Stable with excellent mix	Growing with excellent mix	Growing with poor mix	Growing with fair mix
Stage and store mix (refers to a corridor's size and overall quantity and quality of the corridor's mix)					
Perceptions (refers to leadership, retail mix, cleanliness and safety, importance to immediate community)	Leadership: satisfactory Retail mix: very good Cleanliness/safety: satisfactory Importance: satisfactory	Leadership: very good Retail mix: excellent Cleanliness/safety: very good Importance: excellent	Leadership: marginal Retail mix: excellent Cleanliness/safety: very good Importance: excellent	Leadership: poor Retail mix: poor Cleanliness/safety: marginal Importance: satisfactory	Leadership: very good Retail mix: poor Cleanliness/safety: marginal Importance: satisfactory
Demographic trends (refers to changes in population and impacts between 2000 and 2014 in the corridors)	Latino population decreased by 17.1%, and total also decreased by 14.4%.	Latino population in the increased 12.4%, while the total population decreased by 14.4%	Latino population increased 96%, while the total population increased by 3.8%	Latino population increased 158.1%, and total population increased by +4.9%	Latino population increased 225%, and total population decreased by 2.9%

*Excellent: very strong with some minor weaknesses; very good: strong with numerous minor weaknesses; satisfactory: some strengths but with some moderate weaknesses; marginal: a few strengths and a few major weaknesses; poor: very few strengths and numerous major weaknesses.

examined are responding to social, economic, and demographic changes in the surrounding community. The ethnic supermarkets that anchor many of these corridors are often the only local source of healthy meat and produce in a given neighborhood. Their success has spawned other new retail businesses in the same area. Recognizing the importance of immigrant entrepreneurs in local economies, cities and towns throughout the Rust Belt and beyond have undertaken initiatives to encourage them.

In these corridors, there is tremendous opportunity for place-based community organizations and residents to be champions of economic, social, and cultural development within their neighborhoods. The case studies demonstrate that low-income and minority business owners place a high value on trust, pre-existing relationships, and social capital when seeking support services. Place-based community organizations can develop effective, culturally sensitive trust with low-income and minority business owners while also providing local market knowledge to larger economic development entities. In this sense, their role as local economic developers is critical to the success of any emergent immigrant neighborhood.

The transformation from run-down strip malls to Latino cultural hubs is especially noticeable on weekends when residents come out to do their shopping. Food is an important part of the Latino culture, and ethnic restaurants and ethnic supermarkets have become de facto anchor tenants in retrofitted strip malls. Entire districts are filled with distinct sounds and smells emanating from stores and restaurants along the streets.

The neighborhood commercial corridors presented here cater predominantly to the lowest income bracket of a neighborhood. Most of their patrons are residents who live within walking distance, do not drive, and make less than half the income of their neighbors. The large neighborhood supermarket anchors that are able to offer a more diverse assortment of products and services attract patrons from other neighborhoods or surrounding suburbs. Store location is currently the primary driver in attracting customers. Immigrant groups have tended to settle around commercial cores whose economic activity had peaked in the 1970s and 1980s but thereafter declined. That decline, however, has largely reversed itself in recent years as immigrant entrepreneurs have opened stores and restaurants in vacant and abandoned commercial buildings and stimulated an economic and cultural revitalization. All these case studies have shown that the adaptation process begins when the "big boxes" are vacant and new and small ethnic businesses start moving in to fill those vacancies. The indicators of the success of a corridor include the presence of successful businesses, the availability of reasonably priced goods and services for residents and visitors alike, and the development of a spirit of hope, opportunity, and promise. These indicators and the associated level of economic activity they imply are typically not apparent in the neighborhoods immediately outside the study areas.

Chapter 4

LESSONS AND RECOMMENDATIONS FOR REURBANIZING THE CITY

Conclusions and Implications for Future Planning

The previous chapters in this book have explored approaches that can help us understand why Latino neighborhoods form in large urban areas and identify ways in which these communities contribute to the creation of social, economic, and cultural resiliency for their residents. Latino communities have proven very resilient in adapting to and forming urban neighborhoods that focus on people and place (Lara 2012a,b). Documenting Latinos' influence on communities through cases studies used a three-part approach. The background section (chap. 1) provided an overview of the physical transformation and adaptation of the ethnic corridors under consideration and the research methodology used in their analysis. Chapter 2 explored current and possible future trends in new Latino communities. This section also covered some of the demographic changes in the Latino population in the United States, as well as the social, cultural, and economic ramifications of these changes. Also examined was the important role that Latino entrepreneurs play in their community. Chapter 3 involved conclusions and implications for future planning, focusing on how Latinos are transforming the cultural and economic landscape in derelict and abandoned urban districts and providing recommendations that serve as calls to action for city governments, planners, social groups, and community organizations.

Until very recently, virtually no planning efforts have been carried out by the cities in the study areas, although such efforts have been undertaken by community development and nonprofit organizations. In some of the cases where official city planning has been absent, this neglect has actually helped foster the vibrant, entrepreneurial life that now exists in revitalized neighborhoods. Given the characteristics and conditions of these commercial corridors, one of the lessons for planners, designers, and policy makers is that pre-scriptive planning and design systems do not always yield positive outcomes in the establishment of neighborhoods.

The studied areas represent cases in which planners, design-ers, and policy makers need to step back and take a more enabling approach to planning rather than a prescriptive one. The value and contribution of "bottom-up" processes initiated by local residents and community leaders need to be recognized. In order to avoid the types of mistakes that planners and designers before them have made, they should ask three basic questions in order to implement enabling systems that promote wise planning and help shape an eco-nomically healthy future. First: what are the qualities or set of con-ditions that make this place unique? Second: what interventions are needed to make planning happen more quickly so that the population and tax base are stabilized? Third: what aspects of design need to be addressed in order to create a more inclusive and responsive environ-ment that is, ultimately, a local and regional destination?

Emerging research across the planning and design fields increas-ingly suggests a connection between sustainable urbanism and the cultural and social resiliency of the communities and neighborhoods concerned (Farr 2012; Frank, Engelke, and Schmid 2003; Frumkin, Frank, and Jackson 2013; Gehl 2011; Gehl and Svarre 2013; Glaser 2012; Sucher 2003). A significant gap between knowledge and prac-tice exists, however, with respect to the possible positive impacts of Latino urbanism principles as applied in settings of emergent immi-grant neighborhoods. As the literature review in chapter 2 indicates, whereas Latino urbanism has generally been approached from his-torical, social, and political perspectives, its potential contribution to urban sustainability among immigrant communities has largely been ignored. Recognition and proper implementation of the principles of Latino urbanism represent a tremendous opportunity for enhanced community development. As Latinos are and will continue to be the fastest-growing demographic group within the United States, their engagement in the planning, design, and development of urban com-munities is essential for successful urban sustainability.

The case studies presented in the previous chapter illustrate some of the challenges facing marginalized ethnic communities, as well as the opportunities offered by the principles and practices of

Latino urbanism in building and sustaining economically and culturally resilient communities. The studies demonstrate the effective application of Latino urbanism in fostering culturally, socially, and economically healthy compact communities. Such communities are characterized by a pedestrian-friendly environment with adequate public transportation, and one in which residential and commercial needs mix freely, as evidenced by convenient access to retail shops and ethnic supermarkets offering wholesome meat, produce, and vegetables. These case studies, however, are exceptions to the rule, as Latino urbanism's validation in research has not been matched by any corresponding degree of implementation.

Enabling systems in planning and design policy need to reflect the linkages that exist between immigration and the sustainable physical environment in the following three areas: population growth, neighborhood revitalization, and economic development. Suburban commercial corridors, in general, are changing dramatically in terms of culture, ethnicity, and their demand for urban amenities. These changes are signs of a much larger national transformation of the Latino cultural landscape. Locally, the changes along the McDowell Corridor, the West Vernor–Bagley Street Corridor, the Morse Road and Sullivant Avenue Corridors, and along Indianapolis's West Washington Street are seen against the increasing economic, social, and cultural influence of the Latino community. Cities and neighborhoods are not just physical spaces; they are composed of places that people experience and are representative of a culture. In the case of the study areas, numerous nonprofit organizations and community groups have supported minority businesses, enabling new immigrants to actively participate in the economic transformation of their neighborhoods. This is a consequence of a series of programs funded by public agencies to teach skills in areas such as marketing, business plan development, accounting, information technology, and tax preparation.

Another obvious change in the study areas considered here is the heightened pride community members have in their revitalized neighborhoods. This pride is reflected in new forms of urban space that include imaginative and functional adaptation of underutilized building stock and in an increasing number of organized community festivals and celebrations. The ethnic commercial corridors observed here are just a few of many ethnic-driven urban revitalizations taking place in urban centers in the United States. What were once abandoned, dilapidated and crime-ridden areas are being transformed into dynamic ethnic entrepreneurial centers and destinations located in the heart of major U.S. cities. The goal of planning and design approaches and strategies should be to promote planning and zoning regulations that address the increasing ethnic and cultural diversity of these areas and treat the corridors as unique city attractions. Addressing the quality of life in the revitalization of ethnic commercial corridors requires attention to how neighborhoods function, their cultural history, and how their social forms adapt to and from the urban environment.

Local governments in cites have a crucial role to play in bringing positive change to inner-city areas. They can implement strategic planning and design approaches that provide place-based solutions and promote cultural diversity at all levels. It is crucial to build stakeholder consensus, as without significant support from merchants, community members, and public representatives, it will be difficult to obtain the necessary public and/or private capital any revitalization requires. The entrepreneurial qualities and cultural assets that distinguish Latino communities should be recognized and encouraged at different levels of government as an approach to revitalization.

This analysis has led to the premise that the guiding principles for development should emphasize the formation of meaningful social setting and the focus should be on reconstruction of the city with public spaces. The following recommendations are intended to provide urban planners and designers (whether in the public or private sectors) guidelines for urban revitalization among emergent Latino communities in the United States.

1. CAPITALIZE ON DESTINATIONS AND ATTRACTIONS THAT CELEBRATE THE LOCAL ETHNIC ENTREPRENEURIAL SPIRIT.

It is crucial to identify the qualities or set of conditions that make places unique and to recognize their social and economic value. Embracing the unique character of a location, neighborhood, or community can economically differentiate a project, support asset value, and provide a competitive advantage (Eitler, McMahon, and Thoering 2013). In the study areas presented in the previous chapter, the Latino community had dominated the in-migration trend, with entrepreneurial residents forming an extensive business community. The study areas are characterized by thriving Latino businesses, restaurants, shops, and services. They hold the potential for development of the destination site in a manner that capitalizes on its unique cultural character, enhancing commercial value and increasing its attractiveness to both residents and visitors. A community's attractions are important, as they give potential visitors a motivation to travel there, spend time and money, and return for future visits. Communities that lack attractions are prone to economic decline and disinvestment, with the accompanying liabilities of crime and vandalism. Identity and image are important aspects in the development of a destination's potential attractions. Creation of a positive image may be as simple as a community's commitment to maintaining a clean and physically safe environment. Lighting commercial corridors in a flattering manner may enhance appeal as well, as can showcasing a neighborhood's social and cultural assets.

In addition to identifying destinations and attractions, it is vital to develop and implement planning and design policies that support and enhance ethnic entrepreneurial activity, capital investment, and reinvestment. Targeted investment opportunities along these corridors must be encouraged and supported by nonprofit and public entities. Vacant commercial properties must be reactivated or planned for new development. There are some policy-driven programs that can promote innovation and entrepreneurship (e.g., tax policy and municipal bylaws), but too many of them are not designed with business owners in mind. Planners and policy makers concerned with declining inner-city or suburban retail zones should explore mechanisms that can identify and target areas within cities that are ripe for retrofitting purposes. Cities should supplement the work of local Latino chambers of commerce, nonprofit organizations, and entities in the private sector to promote "third place" small businesses that contribute to the public life in economically depressed areas. It is through "third places" that Latinos effect conversations, exchange concerns, and advise or relate to their fellow citizens, becoming active participants in the daily life of their cities.

City officials should inform merchants of the financial assistance that federal and local programs can provide to those seeking to revitalize inner cities. They should also encourage the establishment of

Figure 27. Examples of destination, cultural identity, and image. (1) Plaza Mexico, Linwood, California; (2) Mexicantown, Detroit; and (3) Broadway Street, Los Angeles. Photos by author.

small neighborhood stores, which provide a crucial retail service besides employing local residents. Latino small businesses provide social, economic, and cultural assets to their communities and contribute to the establishment of a social network. Social networks provide opportunities for interaction among the participants and a sense of belonging. They act as cultural buffers, providing social support and sources of information and referral for economic and medical assistance. Such networks are essential to successfully assimilating immigrants into mainstream society.

Joint ventures between the public and private sectors should be encouraged as well. Local authorities and residents need to understand the social, economic, and cultural implications as they target areas as destination points and commercial magnets for both immigrants and "Main Street" businesses. Some policies should focus on the creation and support of local merchant associations to raise capital (beyond membership dues) to facilitate organizational development and leverage capital to effectively meet the mission of supporting small-business members in their entrepreneurial endeavors. Also, greater consideration should be given to planning and policy tools for preserving and enhancing—or at a minimum, forestalling the closure of—clusters of small neighborhood ethnic businesses. "Buy local" campaigns across the country can encourage greater consumption of a community's own goods and services, keeping income within that community. Centralized entities that can facilitate networking and professional development opportunities are also important forms of support to both prospective and existing business operators. Community connections help entrepreneurs keep track of local trends and remain prepared for new challenges. Immigrants are often hard working and have a desire to succeed, but their networks are often limited and not connected to the broader community. Commercial corridors should be able to identify the "retail gap" within their boundaries and focus on that retail gap. For instance, some of the ethnic commercial corridors have ample excellent neighborhood businesses such as restaurants, fast-food eateries, pharmacies, auto parts and service stores, financial services and banks, and small specialty shops for local residents. In some cases, however, there is a gap or the need in the marketplace for what the industry terms "soft goods," such as clothing, household textiles, and related

Figure 28. Examples of small ethnic businesses that provide social, economic, and cultural comfort to their communities and contribute to the establishment of social networks. (1) West Vernor–Bagley Corridor, southwest Detroit; (2) La Mega Michoacana Market, Morse Road, Columbus; and (3) Mexicantown, Detroit. Photos by author.

products. The leadership in those ethnic commercial corridors should be able to identify the gaps in the marketplace to guarantee a more balanced business environment in the area that will ultimately contribute to the success of the commercial corridor.

2. CAPACITY BUILDING AND UNDERSTANDING THE INTERVENTIONS THAT ARE NEEDED TO MAKE PLANNING HAPPEN.

There is a tremendous need for greater capacity-building support through institutional mechanisms, such as associations that can efficiently coordinate and disseminate information about the regulatory environment, as well as the norms, practices, and politics shaping day-to-day business activities. In addition to capacity building, types of support should include information and referral, training, financing, individualized support, business incubation, and professional networks. Lack of support was stressed by merchants and entrepreneurs in the study areas as the main barrier to starting their own businesses. Merchants and ethnic entrepreneurs have expressed interest in training on how to get their business ventures started. This could include personalized training for those interested in slower-paced self-employment programs as well as more intensive programs. Individualized support should include advice, counseling, and mentoring in a one-on-one format and should be tailored to the needs of each person seeking assistance. This could include programs that cater specifically to people with lower levels of education who seek self-employment and could be achieved through seminars, workshops, and other programs that offer more intensive training in a classroom setting, one that provides opportunities to develop peer networks and receive ongoing guidance and feedback. Also, business incubators aimed at immigrant entrepreneurs and individuals lacking financial resources would help to remove some of the barriers to achieving success. Another idea is to create partnerships between entrepreneurs and underemployed professionals, such as educated youth and skilled immigrants, to help small businesses commercialize new product innovations and services. Another type of partnership is between immigrant entrepreneurs, on the one hand, and native-born business operators and the general entrepreneurship community, on the other. Such a partnership could ensure that immigrant business owners are aware of the resources available in a given place. Opportunities should be created for business operators within a given corridor to share information, strategies, training opportunities, and other resources through the local chamber of commerce and other business organizations. In addition, the creation of "business advocates" can help build community trust. Community trust is essential to the success of ethnic neighborhood businesses. Such trust is necessary when entrepreneurs lack experience in a new environment and where personal relationships must be depended on for support. Place-based organizations can play a significant role in helping new local ethnic businesses integrate into the larger overall commercial sphere. This has been the case in study areas in Detroit and Indianapolis. Ideally, community groups should encourage local business owners to form inclusive business associations dedicated to enhancing the growth and economic empowerment of existing community businesses and entrepreneurs through place-specific support and guidance.

3. THE PHYSICAL ENVIRONMENT NEEDS TO BE ADDRESSED IN URBAN DESIGN IN ANY INCLUSIVE AND RESPONSIVE FORM OF PLANNING.

Architecture and urban design for the project areas should be expressive of the local culture. Greater consideration should be given to planning and policies that preserve and enhance quality of life and the physical environment. The quality of physical spaces and their design is crucial to the success and longevity of any project for urban renewal. Cities need to revisit zoning codes and regulations, all of which should reflect the changing demands and needs of increasingly diverse urban populations. In some communities, zoning and building codes tend to be outdated and to discourage ethnic touches, such as colorfully painted façades, large front porches, fountains, street murals, and wrought-iron fences. The focus should be on the quality of public life and space rather than on specific uses. Improvements in public infrastructure and street amenities are needed to make these areas desirable commercial corridors. Public spaces such as plazas, sidewalks, and pocket parks, which are central elements of the Latino city-building process, should be encouraged throughout districts. Local governments should facilitate redevelopment of vacant and

Figure 29. Examples of architecture that express the character of the local culture. (1) West Vernor–Bagley Corridor, southwest Detroit; (2) Plaza Mexico, Linwood, California; and (3) Mexicantown, southwest Detroit. Photos by author.

neglected properties in areas ripe for revitalization. Cities should also grant low-interest loans and rent subsidies in areas strategically targeted for improvement, while providing incentives for adaptive reuse of obsolete and abandoned buildings and for façade improvements. The names of ethnic commercial corridors need to evoke a positive identity. Organizing community events and street festivals and maintaining a pedestrian-friendly environment would contribute to creating such an identity. Actions that improve the perception and reality of safety must also be encouraged, because people choose to shop and visit where they feel safe. The safety and security of pedestrians and merchants should be an integral part of any area's design guidelines.

The physical organization of space should reflect current demands. The physical organization of commercial space should be oriented around redevelopment nodes or hubs where a community's commercial and/or cultural assets are concentrated. Such is the case with some of the larger ethnic supermarket anchors in the Latino commercial corridors described in the Phoenix, Detroit, and Columbus case studies. Organization of commercial nodes along commercial corridors is important not only to reach optimal market economies of scale, but to provide a sense of place for residents and visitors. Successful commercial nodes are those with high visibility, more often than not located at key intersections accessible to significant levels of pedestrian and vehicular traffic. As activities and services cluster, commercial community hubs develop. Often the impetus for such hubs is a marketplace where meat, produce, vegetables, and other food staples are sold. The communication and gathering involved in the sale and purchase of groceries often forms a social nexus in Latino culture that contributes to community life.

When an individual commercial node becomes specialized to a particular commodity or service, it becomes more attractive to consumers or visitors interested in optimizing their shopping and leisure time.

The most successful retrofitting of ethnic commercial corridors has capitalized on existing linear "strip center" configurations popularized in suburban U.S. settings during the 1970s and 1980s. The single-level "strip center" concept is appealing to immigrant

Figure 30. Examples of architecture that represent businesses arranged around commercial nodes. (1) Indianapolis; (2) McDowell Road, Phoenix; and (3) Indianapolis. Photos by author.

entrepreneurs because of its relatively low construction, maintenance, and leasing costs (Gibbs 2012).

Successful identification and development of commercial nodes in ethnic neighborhoods is best addressed by partnerships between local government officials, business owners, and residents. Some of the most economically viable potential sites may include those that are either vacant or where current structures are significantly underutilized.

Focus energy on streets and sidewalks. Using the ground floors of buildings for commercial activities can increase street and sidewalk activity. The ground floor of a building represents its connection to the rest of the city and to the pedestrians who pass it (Gehl 2013; Glaser 2012). When a building's ground floors are devoted to retail and other nonresidential purposes, social interactions in the adjoining sidewalk area are enhanced and the distinction between public and private space blurs. Optimally, the commercial activities on ground floors should be human scaled and should provide street amenities and infrastructure that will encourage and support diverse type of activities, both necessary and optional. Necessary activities are more or less compulsory; they disregard the quality of public space such as walking or waiting for the bus. Optimal activities require good quality public space and are those in which the user participates if they wish to do so, based on the presence of street amenities. Optimal activities can be passive (seating, waiting) or active (urban recreation) (Gehl 2013). It is critical to recognize that streets and sidewalks are not only a functional environment of the city, but also an environment of experience, and the quality of that experience will depend on the quality of public space. Intuitively, driving or walking by attractive storefronts is a more interesting experience for motorists and pedestrians than passing blank walls. Crowded and bustling sidewalks also promote a greater sense of personal safety than do empty lots and lonely streets.

Ground-floor uses for retail and other activities should spill out onto the sidewalks and streets to blur the distinction between public and private space. The base of a building should be human scaled and allow for interaction between the activities taking place indoors and the pedestrians outside, as active ground-floor uses can create valuable experiences along a street for both pedestrians and motorists. Heightened transparency through large windows and doors further

Figure 31. Examples of visual connections at the street level. (1) and (2) Mexicantown, southwest Detroit; (3) McDowell Road, Phoenix. Photos by author.

acts to slow vehicular traffic, just as it encourages pedestrian and consequent commercial activity. This phenomenon was observed in some of the study areas presented in chapter 3.

A ground floor of a structure represents a nexus or "edge" to the outside where a visual connection to passersby can be offered that allows them to enjoy the aesthetics and activities of the indoor space. Such edges should be active year-round and unite both sides of the street. The visual connection contributes to the character, image, and identity of a given place. The closer we get to buildings, the more they become part of our experience. If the ground floors of a building are interesting and inviting, the urban experience of which it is part is enriched; if the ground floors are closed or lack detail and interest, the urban experience remains flat and impersonal (Gehl 2011; Gehl and Svarre 2013; Glaser 2012; Sucher 2003).

Emphasis should be placed on public spaces. Energizing a community's shared spaces will lead to a higher quality of public space. One of the points demonstrated in the case studies was that "third places" and public spaces are an important part of daily life in emergent immigrant neighborhoods because they not only provide residents with a place to relax and unwind from the stresses of home and work, but also act as buffer zones during the assimilation process. In Latin American cultures third places and public spaces are a priority in urban design and architecture. On the other hand, in the United States, third places and public spaces have never been so significant, perhaps because of the lack of economic, demographic, and political centralization that has characterized the country's development. It must be noted, however, that a lack of public space (or effective transportation options that encourages its use) has been correlated with poorer physical and mental health and the higher medical costs associated with this. Loneliness, depression, and anxiety can all stem from social isolation (Eitler, McMahon, and Thoering 2013; Frank, Engelke, and Schmid 2003; Frumkin, Frank, and Jackson 2013).

Analysis of the public realm in case studies revealed when public or third places are not formally present in the urban fabric, Latino immigrants may culturally adapt or transform spaces. Nontraditional settings, such as sidewalks, ethnic markets, food trucks, convenience stores, or butcher shops, become third places where individuals not only purchase a product or service but congregate for social purposes.

Figure 32. Examples of architecture that represent energized shared spaces. (1) and (2) West Vernor–Bagley Corridor, southwest Detroit; (3) Broadway Street, Los Angeles. Photos by author.

Successful urban design includes attention to features that encourage social interaction. A starting point might be to map a community's existing assets to identify communal open spaces that might provide opportunities for physical activity and social engagement otherwise lacking. The mapping can help prioritize those areas where improvements and required investments could best be made to respond to socioeconomic and/or demographic changes. For example, a place where a disproportionate number of residents gather to purchase a product or service might be an effective point for a strategic planning intervention.

Reconquer the sidewalk and invest in amenities. Sidewalks and street amenities support a variety of activities in emergent immigrant neighborhoods. Sidewalks create the first and last impressions when visiting commercial areas in ethnic neighborhoods. Shoppers and visitors investing time in walking and patronizing businesses expect a pleasant and comfortable experience, which includes attractive storefronts and sidewalks of sufficient width to accommodate easy movement, as well as outside displays and street-side dining (Gibbs 2012). Attractive pedestrian thoroughfares accompanied by appropriate amenities, along with colors and artwork particular to a given culture, can reinforce a positive cultural identity and image for a location, as well as instill pride among residents. Examples of appropriate amenities include adequate and attractive waste receptacles assuring cleanliness, drinking fountains, adequate street lighting to maintain safety, bicycle racks, a sufficient number of public benches for seating, and a sufficient number of food vendors. Research has indicated that the level of street activity in a commercial area is largely a function of the amenities provided. Where the quality of a public space is high, optional activities such as reading, eating, talking, and simply relaxing are more likely to occur (Gehl 2011; Gehl and Svarre 2013; Oldenburg 2001; Sucher 2003).

Urban life in the public realm is constantly changing in both character and purpose, and planners, designers, and policy makers need to be sensitive to such changes. Amenities need to support both "passive" and "active" activities, whether it be sitting on a stairstep or bench to watch passersby, dining at an outdoor café, or jogging or skateboarding down a city street. Streets in emergent immigrant neighborhoods are more than a means of travel; they are a primary

Figure 33. Examples of reconquered sidewalks with complementary amenities. (1) Broadway Street, Los Angeles; (2) West Vernor–Bagley Corridor, southwest Detroit; and (3) Plaza Mexico, Linwood, California. Photos by author.

form of public space. Communities should recognize the concept of the "living street" where appropriate. A living street is a street that has been planned and designed principally for social interactions: a place where people can meet and children can play in a safe and welcoming environment.

While there is no single solution for countering urban decline, entrepreneurial immigrants have proven to have a positive impact on population growth, economic development, and neighborhood revitalization. Likewise, strategies and approaches that incorporate the guiding principles of Latino urbanism have contributed to the creation of healthier and more desirable communities. This is because cities are better understood through piecemeal inspection and analysis of their separate districts. Strategically located projects in a neighborhood can foster the development of culturally relevant public space, enhance commercial values, and create pride among residents.

As discussed in earlier chapters, Latino culture places emphasis on family values, social networks, and the use of public open space for large gatherings, and these elements are critical at all levels in the revitalization process. Foreign-born entrepreneurs locating along at-risk commercial corridors in cities and suburbs across the country are investing in vacant and neglected properties and reinvigorating neighborhoods. Immigrant-operated businesses provide much-needed goods and services to underserved immigrant populations, revitalize neglected urban infrastructure, and contribute to community vitality and placemaking. To realize the full potential of derelict and decaying commercial corridors, community economic development strategies should support the transformation of immigrant commercial corridors by assisting with capital acquisition, altering zoning laws, and by teaching about and allowing for capacity building. Most importantly, there should be reforms that provide immigrants and the communities in which they live with the tools to prosper.

APPENDIX

Case Studies GIS

Boundary Selection Criteria

1. The basic unit of population data is at the census block group level.
2. In ArcGIS, using a census block group shapefile, a centroid of each census block group is created (only inside).
3. Only those census block groups whose centroids are within two miles of the corridor of interest are selected.
4. However, not all these selected block groups are included in the final analysis. Since the size and shape of census block group polygons are quite variable, I went through an additional editing process where I manually excluded a few polygons. For example, if the polygon of a census block group is very large, most of the area it covers may not be accessible within two miles of the corridor.
5. Thus, I created a buffer polygon of two miles from the corridor and then manually excluded a polygon unless more than 70 percent of its area is covered by the buffer area (visually determined).

Data Source

1. American FactFinder (U.S. Census Bureau): http://factfinder.census.gov/faces/nav/jsf/pages/searchresults.xhtml?refresh=t.
2. "TIGER Products" (U.S. Census Bureau): http://www.census.gov/geo/maps-data/data/tiger.html.
3. "Geolytics," 2000 long-form data normalized into 2010 Census block group boundaries: 2000, 2010 Dataset (State, County, and Block group); 2000, 2010 *Census Summary File 1* (SF1 100%), e.g., *Total Population & Hispanic or Latino Origin (of any race)—2010 SF1 100% Data*; 2014 Dataset (State, County, and Block group) 2010–2014 ACS (American Community Survey) 5-Year Estimates; last updated: Yujin Park, March 8, 2017.

BIBLIOGRAPHY

Acosta, G. 2013. *State of Hispanic Homeownership Report for 2013.* San Diego: National Association of Hispanic Real Estate Professionals.

Agius, V. J. 2012. *Barrios to Burbs: The Making of the Mexican-American Middle Class.* Stanford, Calif.: Stanford University Press.

Akoukou, M. 2015. "The Crossroads of America: How Indianapolis Has Benefited from Booming Latino Business Community." *Latin Post.* http://www.latinpost.com/articles /43251/20150428/crossroads-america-indianapolis-earned-new-nickname-due -booming-local-latino.htm.

Altman, I., and S. M. Low. 1992. *Place Attachment.* New York: Plenum Press.

Alvarado, R. 2003. *Mexicans and Mexican Americans in Michigan.* East Lansing: Michigan State University Press.

American Immigration Council. 2015. "New Americans in Indiana." American Immigration Council, January 1. http://www.immigrationpolicy.org/just-facts/new-americans-indiana.

America's Voice. 2010. "The Power of the Latino Vote in the 2010 Elections: They Tipped Elections in 2008; Where Will They Be in 2101?" http://www.sph.sc.edu/cli /documents/ee14c7a86ad579874c_o0m6ivfoa.pdf.

Anderson, M. 2016. "Who Relies on Public Transit in the U.S." Pew Research Center, August 7. http://www.pewresearch.org/fact-tank/2016/04/07/who-relies-on-public-transit-in -the-u-s/.

Angotti, T. 2012. "Placemaking in New York City: From Puerto Rican to Pan-Latino." In *Diálogos: Placemaking in Latino Communities,* edited by M. Rios, L. Vazquez, and L. Miranda, 113–25. Milton Park, Abingdon: Routledge.

Armas, A., A, McCaskill, and R. Roussell. 2017. "Latina 2.0: Fiscally Conscious, Culturally Influential, and Familia Forward." Nielsen, September 12. http://www.nielsen.com /content/dam/corporate/us/en/reports-downloads/2017-reports/Latina%202.0.pdf.

Arnold, D., and J. Turrin. 2012. "West Washington Commercial Corridor Technical Assessment." http://csl.iupui.edu/doc/final-report-west-washington.pdf.

Aronson, David. 1997. "Immigrant Entrepreneurs." *Research Perspectives on Migration* 1 (2).

Arreola, D. D., ed. 2005. *Hispanic Spaces, Latino Places: Community and Cultural Diversity in Contemporary America.* Austin: University of Texas Press.

———. 2012. "Placemaking and Latino Urbanism in a Phoenix Mexican Immigrant Community." *Journal of Urbanism: International Research on Placemaking and Urban Sustainability* 5 (2–3): 157–70.

Banerjee, T. 2001. "The Future of Public Space." *Journal of the American Planning Association* 67 (1): 9.

Barajas, J., D. Chatman, and A. Weinstein. (2016). "Exploring Bicycle and Public Transit Use by Low-Income Latino Immigrants: A Mixed-Methods Study in the San Francisco Bay Area." San José, Calif.: Mineta Transportation Institute. http://transweb.sjsu.edu /PDFs/research/1202-bicycle-and-transit-use-by-low-income-latino-immigrants.pdf.

Barreto, M. A., and G. M. Segura. 2014. *Latino America: How America's Most Dynamic Population Is Poised to Transform the Politics of the Nation.* New York: PublicAffairs.

Beatley, T. 2004. *Native to Nowhere: Sustaining Home and Community in a Global Age.* Washington, D.C.: Island Press.

Beatley, T., and K. Manning. 1997. *Beyond the New Urbanism: Planning for Environment, Economy, and Community*. Washington, D.C.: Island Press.

Bernardo, R. 2014. "2014's Best and Worst Cities for Hispanic Entrepreneurs." https://wallethub.com/edu/best-and-worst-cities-for-hispanic-entrepreneurs/6491/.

Bernstein, N. 2005. "Record Immigration Is Changing the Face of New York's Neighborhoods." *New York Times*, January 24, p. A1.

Bohl, C. C. 2000. "New Urbanism and the City: Potential Applications and Implications for Distressed Inner-City Neighborhoods. *Housing Policy Debate* 11 (4): 761–801.

Briggs de Souza, X. 1998. "Brown Kids in White Suburbs: Housing Mobility and the Many Faces of Social Capital." *Housing Policy Debate* 9 (1): 177–221.

Bureau of Labor Statistics. 2012. *The Latino Labor Force at a Glance*. Washington, D.C.: U.S. Department of Labor.

Calderon, M., and A. Becerra. 2016. *2016 State of Hispanic Homeownership Report*. Hispanic Wealth Project, October 6. http://hispanicwealthproject.org/state-of-hispanic-homeownership-report/.

Calthorpe, P., and W. Fulton. 2001. *The Regional City: Planning for the End of Sprawl*. Washington, D.C.: Island Press.

Card, D. 2007. "How Immigration Affects U.S. Cities." Discussion Paper Series, CDP No. 11/07. London: Centre for Research and Analysis of Migration.

Cardenas, V., S. Kerby, and R. Wilf. 2012. "Arizona's Demographic Changes: A Look at the State's Emerging Communities of Color." Center for American Progress, February 28. http://www.americanprogress.org/issues/poverty/news/2012/02/28/11060/arizonas-demographic-changes/.

Carlile, W. H. 1997. "All Anglo No More, a Latin Phoenix Rises." *Las Vegas Sun*, August 2003. https://lasvegassun.com/news/1997/aug/05/all-anglo-no-more-a-latin-phoenix-rises/.

Carmona, M., and S. Tiesdell. 2007. *Urban Design Reader*. Boston: Architectural Press.

Carpio, G., C. Irazábal, and L. Pulido. 2011. "The Right to the Suburb? Rethinking Lefebvre and Immigrant Activism." *Journal of Urban Affairs* 33 (2): 185–208.

Cartagena, C. 2013. *Latino Boom II: Catch the Biggest Demographic Wave Since the Baby Boom*. New York: Worthy Shorts, Inc.

Castro, J. 2013. "Myths About Affluent Hispanic Households." http://adage.com/article/the-big-tent/myths-affluent-hispanic-households/144248/.

Chase, J., M. Crawford, and J. Kaliski. 1999. *Everyday Urbanism: Featuring John Chase*. New York: Monacelli Press.

———. 2009. *Everyday Urbanism*. New York: Monacelli Press.

Chavis, D., and A. Wandersman. 1990. "Sense of Community in the Urban Environment: A Catalyst for Participation and Community Development." *American Journal of Community Psychology* 18 (1): 55–67.

Chen, Q., C. Acey, and J. Lara. 2015. "Sustainable Futures for Linden Village: A Model for Increasing Social Capital and the Quality of Life in an Urban Neighborhood." *Sustainable Cities and Society* 14: 359–73.

Cisneros, H., and J. Rosales. 2006. *Casa y Comunidad: Latino Home and Neighborhood Design*. Washington, D.C.: BuilderBooks.com.

Cohen, D., J. Passel, and M. Lopez. 2011. "Census 2010: 50 Million Latinos, Hispanics Account for More than Half of Nation's Growth in Past Decade." Pew Hispanic Research Center, March 24. http://www.pewhispanic.org/2011/03/24/hispanics-account-for-more-than-half-of-nations-growth-in-past-decade/.

Cohen, L., A. Iton, R. Davis, and S. Rodriguez. 2009. *A Time of Opportunity: Local Solutions to Reduce Inequities in Health and Safety*. Prevention Institute, May. http://www.preventioninstitute.org/component/jlibrary/article/id-81/127.html.

Coleman, J. 1988. "Social Capital and the Creation of Human Capital." *American Journal of Sociology* 94 (suppl.): S95–S120.

Condon, M., and R. Yaro. 2010. *Seven Rules for Sustainable Communities: Design Strategies for the Post-carbon World*. Washington, D.C.: Island Press.

Conover, J., C. Rogers, and M. Kinghorn. 2005. *Indiana's Latino Population: Demographic and Economic Perspectives*. Prepared by the Indiana Business Research Center, Kelly School of Business, Indiana University. http://www.ibrc.indiana.edu/briefs/Latinos -Apr07.pdf.

Davila, A. M. 2004. *Barrio Dreams: Puerto Ricans, Latinos, and the Neoliberal City*. Berkeley: University of California Press.

Davis, M. 2001. *Magical Urbanism: Latinos Reinvent the US City*. London: Verso.

Degler, C. 1984. *Out of Our Past: The Forces That Shaped Modern America*. 3rd ed. New York: Harper.

Delgado, M. 1997. "Role of Latina-Owned Beauty Parlors in a Latino Community." *Social Work* 42 (5): 445–53.

———. 2007. *Social Work with Latinos: A Cultural Assets Paradigm*. Oxford: Oxford University Press.

———. 2011. *Latino Small Businesses and the American Dream: Community Social Work Practice and Economic and Social Development*. New York: Columbia University Press.

Diaz, D. R. 2005. *Barrio Urbanism: Chicanos, Planning, and American Cities*. New York: Routledge.

Diaz, D. R., and R. D. Torres. 2012. *Latino Urbanism: The Politics of Planning, Policy, and Redevelopment*. New York: New York University Press.

Dieterlen, S. L. 2015. *Immigrant Pastoral: Midwestern Landscapes and Mexican-American Neighborhoods*. New York: Routledge.

Dunham-Jones, E., and J. Williamson. (2011). *Retrofitting Suburbia: Urban Design Solutions for Redesigning Suburbs*. Hoboken, N.J.: Wiley.

Eisenach, J. 2016. "Making America Rich Again: The Latino Effect on Economic Growth." NERA Economic Consulting, December. http://www.nera.com/content/dam/nera /publications/2016/PUB_LDC_Prosperity_1216.pdf.

Eitler, R., E. McMahon, and T. Thoering. 2013. "Ten Principles for Building Healthy Communities." Washington, D.C.: Urban Land Institute. http://uli.org/wp-content /uploads/ULI-Documents/10-Principles-for-Building-Healthy-Places.pdf.

Ellin, N. 2006. *Integral Urbanism*. New York: Routledge.

Erickson, D. 2007. *Expanding the Corktown-Mexicantown Greenlink: Connecting Southwest Neighbors*. Healthy Environments Partnerships. http://www.hepdetroit.org/images /PDFs/report-swgreenway.pdf.

Eroglu, S. 2002. "Impact of Ethnic Minority Retailers on Urban Revitalization Efforts: The Buford Corridor Case." *Journal of Shopping Center Research* 9 (2): 53–75.

Farr, D. 2012. *Sustainable Urbanism: Urban Design with Nature*. Hoboken, N.J.: Wiley.

Ferenchik, M. 2010. "Latinos, Asians Log Big Growth." *Columbus Dispatch*, July 20. http:// www.dispatch.com/content/stories/local/2010/05/09/latinos-asians-log-big-growth .html.

Fishman, R. 2005. "Longer View: The Fifth Migration." *Journal of the American Planning Association* 71 (4): 357–66.

Flippen, C. A., and E. A. Parrado. 2012. "Forging Hispanic Communities in New Destinations: A Case Study of Durham, North Carolina. *City and Community* 11 (1): 1–30.

Francis, M. 1999. *A Case Study Method for Landscape Architecture*. Washington, D.C.: Landscape Architecture Foundation.

Frank, L. D., P. O. Engelke, and T. L. Schmid. 2003. *Health and Community Design: The Impact of the Built Environment on Physical Activity*. 2nd ed. Washington, D.C.: Island Press.

Frey, W. 2001. *Melting Pot Suburbs: A Census 2000 Study of Suburban Diversity*. Brookings, June 1. https://www.brookings.edu/wp-content/uploads/2016/06/frey.pdf.

Frumkin, H., L. Frank, and R. Jackson. 2013. *Urban Sprawl and Public Health: Designing, Planning, and Building for Healthy Communities*. Washington, D.C: Island Press.

Fry, R. 2008. *Latino Settlement in the New Century*. Washington, D.C.: Pew Hispanic Center.

Gámez, J. L. 2002. "Representing the City: The Imagination and Critical Practice in East Los Angeles." *Aztlan* 27 (1): 95–120.

Gammage, G. 2003. *Phoenix in Perspective: Reflection on Developing the Desert*. Tempe, Ariz.: Herberger Center for Design Excellence, College of Architecture and Environmental Design, Arizona State University.

Gehl, J. 2011. *Life Between Buildings: Using Public Space*. Washington, D.C.: Island Press.

———. 2013. *Cities for People*. Washington, D.C.: Island Press.

Gehl, J., and S. Svarre. 2013. *How to Study Public Life*. Washington, D.C.: Island Press.

Ghose, C. 2010. "Ethnic Businesses Ending Vacancies." *Columbus Business First*, August 24. http://www.bizjournals.com/columbus/stories/2010/08/23/story2.html?page=all.

Ghosh, B. 2010. "Arab-Americans: Detroit's Unlikely Saviors." *Time*, November 13. http://content.time.com/time/magazine/article/0,9171,2028057,00.html.

Gibbs, R. J. 2012. *Principles of Urban Retail Planning and Development*. Hoboken, N.J.: Wiley.

Gibson, C. R. 2010. "Place Making: Mapping Culture, Creating Places: Collisions of Science and Art." *Local-Global: Identity, Security, Community* 7: 66–83.

Gil, L. 2013. "Five Reasons Why Upscale Latinos Represent the Next Market Boom." *Fox News Latino*, April 4. http://latino.foxnews.com/latino/opinion/2013/06/11/five-reasons-why-upscale-latinos-represent-next-market-boom/.

Glaser, M. 2012. *The City at Eye Level: Lessons for Street Plinths*. Delft: Eburon.

González, E. 2017. *Latino City: Urban Planning, Politics, and the Grassroots*. London: Routledge.

González, E., and R. Lejano. 2009. "New Urbanism and the Barrio." *Environment and Planning A* 41 (12): 2946–63.

González, E., S. Sarmiento, S. Urzua, and C. Luévano. 2012. "The Grassroots and New Urbanism: A Case from a Southern California Latino Community." *Journal of Urbanism* 5 (2–3): 219–39.

Goździak, E. M., and S. F. Martin. 2005. *Beyond the Gateway: Immigrants in a Changing America*. Lanham, Md.: Lexington Books.

Greene, R. 1995. "Chicago's New Immigrants, Indigenous Poor, and Edge Cities." *Annals of the American Academy of Political and Social Science* 551 (1997): 178–90.

Groth, P. E., and T. W. Bressi. 1997. *Understanding Ordinary Landscapes*. New Haven, Conn.: Yale University Press.

Hall, E. T. 1990. *The Hidden Dimension*. New York: Anchor Books.

Halter, M. 1995. *New Migrants in the Marketplace: Boston's Ethnic Entrepreneurs*. Amherst: University of Massachusetts Press.

Haltiwanger, J. 2012. "Job Creation and Firm Dynamics in the United States." *Innovation Policy and the Economy* 12 (1): 17–38.

Hanchett, T. 2010. "Salad-Bowl Suburbs: A History of Charlotte's East Side and South Boulevard Immigrant Corridors." http://www.historysouth.org/saladbowl/.

Harris, D. 2008. "Shepherding Success: Chamber Works to Help Hispanic Businesses Grow." *Az Business*, September 1. https://azbigmedia.com/help-hispanic-businesses-grow/.

Harvey, D. 1997. "The New Urbanism and the Communitarian Trap." *Harvard Design Magazine*, Winter/Spring. http://www.harvarddesignmagazine.org/issues/1/the-new -urbanism-and-the-communitarian-trap.

Hayden, D. 1995. *The Power of Place: Urban Landscapes as Public History*. Cambridge, Mass.: MIT Press.

Hayduk, D. 1998. *Immigration, Race, and Community Revitalization*. Washington, D.C.: Project on Structural Racism and Community Revitalization, Aspen Institute.

Herzog, L. A. 2006. *Return to the Center: Culture, Public Space, and City Building in a Global Era*. Austin: University of Texas Press.

The Hispanic Population of Southeast Michigan: Characteristics and Economic Contributions. 2008. Wayne State University Center for Urban Studies and the Hispanic Business Alliance. http://www.cus.wayne.edu/media/1563/hispaniccontributionstosem.pdf.

Humphreys, J. M. 2008. "The Multicultural Economy 2008." *Georgia Business and Economic Conditions* 68 (3): 1–16. http://www.terry.uga.edu/selig/docs/GBEC0803q.pdf.

———. 2013. *The Multicultural Economy 2013*. Athens, Ga.: Selig Center for Economic Growth, Terry College of Business, University of Georgia.

———. 2014. "The Multicultural Economy 2014." Selig Center for Economic Growth, Terry College of Business, University of Georgia.

Hwang, J., and R. J. Sampson. 2014. "Divergent Pathways of Gentrification: Racial Inequality and the Social Order of Renewal in Chicago Neighborhoods." *American Sociological Review* 79 (4): 726–51.

Immigration Policy Center. 2013. "New Americans in Ohio: The Political and Economic Power of Immigrants, Latinos, and Asians in the Buckeye State." *American Immigration Council*. http://www.immigrationpolicy.org/sites/default/files/docs/ohio _entrepreneurship_1.pdf.

Irazábal, C. 2009. "One Size Does Not Fit All: Land Markets and Property Rights for the Construction of the Just City." *International Journal of Urban and Regional Research* 33 (2): 558–63.

———, ed. 2014. *Transbordering Latin Americas: Liminal Places, Cultures, and Powers (T) Here*. New York: Routledge.

Irazábal, C., and R. Farhat. 2012. "Historical Overview of Latinos and Planning in the Southwest, 1900 to Present." In *Diálogos: Placemaking in Latino Communities*, edited by M. Rios, L. Vazquez, and L. Miranda. Milton Park, Abingdon: Routledge.

Irazábal, C., and M. Gómez-Barris. 2007. "Bounded Tourism: Immigrant Politics, Consumption, and Traditions at Plaza Mexico." *Journal of Tourism and Cultural Change* 5 (3): 186–213.

ITEP (Institute on Taxation and Economic Policy). 2013. "Undocumented Immigrants' State and Local Tax Contributions." Institute of Taxation and Economic Policy, March 2. http://www.itep.org/pdf/undocumentedtaxes.pdf.

Jacobs, A. B. 1993. *Great Streets*. Cambridge, Mass.: MIT Press.

Jacobs, J. 1992. *The Death and Life of Great American Cities*. New York: Vintage Books.

Kaplan, D. H., and W. Li. 2006. *Landscapes of the Ethnic Economy*. Lanham, Md.: Rowman and Littlefield.

Kayitsinga, J. 2007. *Demography Report Number 1*. Lansing: T.J.S.R. Institute, Michigan State University.

Khojasteh, M., and S. Raja. 2016. "Agents of Change: How Immigrant-Run Ethnic Food Retailers Improve Food Environments." *Journal of Hunger and Environmental Nutrition* 36: 1–29.

Kim, S. 2012. "On Fences, Plazas, and Latino Urbanism: A Conversation with James Rojas." *Folklife Magazine*, October 6. https://folklife.si.edu/talkstory/2015/on-fences-plazas -and-latino-urbanism-a-conversation-with-james-rojas.

Kinghorn, M. 2008. "Indiana Population Projections by Race and Hispanic Origin." *InContext* 9 (8). Indiana Business Research Center, Kelley School of Business, Indiana University. http://www.incontext.indiana.edu/2008/sept-oct/1.asp.

Kinninger, B., and N. Martin. 2014. *Northland Visioning: A Connected Community*. Service Learning Community Design Studio, City and Regional Planning. Knowlton School of Architecture, Ohio State University.

Kneebone, E., and E. Holmes. 2015. "The Growing Distance Between People and Jobs in Metropolitan America." Brookings, March 24. https://www.brookings.edu/research/the-growing-distance-between-people-and-jobs-in-metropolitan-america/.

Knox, P. L. 1993. *The Restless Urban Landscape*. Englewood Cliffs, N.J.: Prentice Hall.

Kostof, S., and R. Tobias. 2003. *The City Shaped: Urban Patterns and Meanings Through History*. Boston: Bullfinch Press.

Kotin, S., G. R. Dyrness, and C. Irazábal. 2011. "Immigration and Integration: Religious and Political Activism for/with Immigrants in Los Angeles." *Progress in Development Studies* 11 (4): 263–84.

Krogstad, M., and A. Flores. 2016. "Unlike Other Latinos, About Half of Cuban Voters in Florida Backed Trump." Pew Research Institute, November 15. http://www.pewresearch.org/fact-tank/2016/11/15/unlike-other-latinos-about-half-of-cuban-voters-in-florida-backed-trump/.

Kunstler, J. H. 1994. *The Geography of Nowhere: The Rise and Decline of America's Man-Made Landscape*. New York: Simon and Schuster.

Kyvig, D. E., and M. A. Marty. 2000. *Nearby History: Exploring the Past Around You*. Walnut Creek, Calif.: AltaMira Press.

Lacey, M. 2010. "Hispanics Are Surging in Arizona." *New York Times*, March 10. http://www.nytimes.com/2011/03/11/us/11arizona.html?_r=0.

Lara, J. 2012a. "Latino Urbanism: Placemaking in 21st-Century American Cities." *Journal of Urbanism: International Research on Placemaking and Urban Sustainability* 5: 95–100.

———. 2012b. "Patterns and Forms of Latino Cultural Landscapes: Southwest Detroit, a Case of Incremental Re-adaptive Use." *Journal of Urbanism: International Research on Placemaking and Urban Sustainability* 5 (2–3): 139–56.

Larget, M., M. Schulz, and J. Schwieterman. 2013. *The Store Next Door: How Ethnic Grocery Stores Contribute to Neighborhood Life and Cross-cultural Food Consumption in Chicago*. Chaddick Institute for Metropolitan Development, DePaul University. https://las.depaul.edu/centers-and-institutes/chaddick-institute-for-metropolitan-development/research-and-publications/Documents/The%20Store%20Next%20Door_03.19.13.pdf.

Latorre, G. 2009. *Walls of Empowerment*. Austin: University of Texas Press.

Lejano, P., and E. González. 2017. "Sorting Through Differences." *Journal of Planning Education and Research* 37 (1): 5–17.

Levitt, P. 1995. "*A Todos les Llamo Primo* (I Call Everyone Cousin): The Social Basis for Latino Small Businesses." In *New Migrants in the Marketplace: Boston's Ethnic Entrepreneurs*, edited by M. Halter, 120–39. Amherst: University of Massachusetts Press.

Littlepage, L. 2006. "Latino Population Boom Impacts Indianapolis." Center for Urban Policy and the Environment, January. http://policyinstitute.iu.edu/uploads/PublicationFiles/157_06-C01.pdf.

Logan, R. 2003. *America's Newcomers*. Albany, N.Y.: Lewis Mumford Center for Comparative Urban and Regional Research, University of Albany.

Londoño, J. 2010. "Latino Design in an Age of Neoliberal Multiculturalism: Contemporary Changes in Latin/o American Urban Cultural Representation." *Identities: Global Studies in Culture and Power* 17 (5): 487–509.

Lopez, G. 2015. "Hispanics of Cuban Origin in the United States, 2013." *Pew Research Center*, September 15. http://www.pewhispanic.org/2015/09/15/hispanics-of-cuban-origin-in-the-united-states-2013/.

Lopez, M. 2012. "A Record 24 Million Latinos Are Eligible to Vote, but Turnout Rate Has Lagged That of Whites, Blacks." Pew Research Center, October 1. http://www.pewhispanic.org/2012/10/01/a-record-24-million-latinos-are-eligible-to-vote/.

Loukaitou-Sideris, A. 1995. "Urban Form and Social Context: Cultural Differentiation in the Uses of Urban Parks." *Journal of Planning Education and Research* 14 (2): 89–102.

Loukaitou-Sideris, A., and T. Banerjee. 1998. *Urban Design Downtown: Poetics and Politics of Form*. Berkeley: University of California Press.

Low, S., and S. Smith. 2006. *The Politics of Public Space*. New York: Routledge.

Lynch, K. 1960. *The Image of the City*. Cambridge, Mass.: MIT Press.

Malavé, I., and E. Giordani. 2014. *Latino Stats: American Hispanics by the Numbers*. New York: New Press.

Marcuse, P. 2000. "The New Urbanism: The Dangers So Far." *disP—The Planning Review* 36 (140): 4–6.

Massey, D. 1986. "The Settlement Process Among Mexican Migrants to the United States." *American Sociological Review* 51 (5): 670–84.

McDaniel, P. 2014. "Revitalization in the Heartland of America: Welcoming Immigrant Entrepreneurs for Economic Development." Washington, D.C.: American Immigration Council.

McTaggart, J. 2004. "Supermarkets: The Latino Influence." *Hispanic Trending*, October 15. http://juantornoe.blogs.com/hispanictrending/2004/10/supermarkets_th.html.

Meinig, D., J. Wand, and B. Jackson. 1979. *The Interpretation of Ordinary Landscapes: Geographical Essays*. New York: Oxford University Press.

Mendez, M. 2005. "Latino New Urbanism: Building on Cultural Preferences." *Opolis: An International Journal of Suburban and Metropolitan Studies* 1 (1): 33–48.

Mendez, M. A. 2003. *Latino Lifestyle and the New Urbanism: Synergy Against Sprawl*. Master's thesis, Massachusetts Institute of Technology.

Mitchell, W. J. 1996. *City of Bits: Space, Place, and the Infobahn*. Cambridge, Mass.: MIT Press.

Myers, D. 1999. "Immigration: Fundamental Force in the American City." *Housing Facts and Findings* 1 (4): 3–5.

Nataly, K. 2013. "Univision's Ratings Win Underlines the Power of Hispanic Marketing." *Harvard Business Review*, August 5. http://blogs.hbr.org/2013/08/univisions-ratings-win-underli/.

New America Alliance Institute. 2014. *American Latino Agenda Report 2014*. http://d3n8a8pro7vhmx.cloudfront.net/themes/5307deb3ebad647150000002/attachments/original/1407257495/2014_American_Latino_Agenda_Report.pdf?1407257495.

Nielsen Company. 2012. *State of the Hispanic Consumer: The Hispanic Market Imperative*. Report, Quarter 2.

———. 2013. *Latina Power Shift*. https://www.iab.com/wp-content/uploads/2015/08/Nielsen_Latina_Report_2013_.pdf.

Noriega, J., and E. Blair. 2008. "Advertising to Bilinguals: Does the Language of Advertising Influence the Nature of Thoughts?" *Journal of Marketing* 72 (5): 69–83.

NPD Group. 2013. "Understand Your Competition and Improve Product Launch Results."

Oberle, A. 2004. "Se Venden Aquí: Latino Commercial Landscapes in Phoenix, Arizona." In *Hispanic Spaces, Latino Places: Community and Cultural Diversity in Contemporary America*, edited by D. Arreola, 239–54. Austin: University of Texas Press.

———. 2006. "Latino Business Landscapes and the Hispanic Ethnic Economy." In *Landscapes of the Ethnic Economy*, edited by D. Kaplan and W. Li, 149–63. New York: Rowman and Littlefield.

Odem, M., and E. Cantrell Lacy. 2009. *Latino Immigrants and the Transformation of the U.S. South*. Athens: University of Georgia Press.

Oldenburg, R. 2001. *Celebrating the Third Place: Inspiring Stories About the "Great Good Places" at the Heart of Our Communities*. New York: Marlowe and Co.

Onésimo, S. J. S., and J. Jennings. 2012. "Barrios and Hyper Barrios: How Latino Neighborhoods Changed the Urban Built Environment." *Journal of Urbanism: International Research on Placemaking and Urban Sustainability* 5: 111–38.

Ong, P. M., and A. Loukaitou-Sideris. 2006. *Jobs and Economic Development in Minority Communities*. Philadelphia: Temple University Press.

Oosting, J. 2010. "Must-Read Report: Detroit's 48217 Zip Code Is Michigan's Most Polluted." *MLive*, June 21. http://www.mlive.com/news/detroit/index.ssf/2010/06/must-read_report_detroits_4821.html?utm_source=feedburner&utm_medium=feed&utm_campaign=Feed%3A+detroit-news+%28Detroit+News+-+MLive.com%29.

Project for Public Spaces. 2017. "What Is Placemaking?" Project for Public Spaces. http://www.pps.org/articles/what_is_placemaking/.

Putnam, R. 2000. *Bowling Alone: The Collapse and Revival of American Community*. London: Simon and Schuster.

Ramati, R. 1981. *How to Save Your Own Street*. Garden City, N.Y.: Dolphin Books.

Rex, T. 2011. *The Latino Population in Arizona: Growth, Characteristics, and Outlook—with a Focus on Latino Education*. Tempe, Ariz.: Center for Competitiveness and Prosperity Research, L. William Seidman Research Institute, W. P. Carey School of Business, Arizona State University. http://hdl.handle.net/2286/R.I.15461.

Rios, M. 2009. "Public Space Praxis: Cultural Capacity and Political Efficacy in Latina/o Placemaking." *Berkeley Planning Journal* 22: 92–112.

Rios, M., L. Vazquez, and L. Miranda. 2012. *Diálogos: Placemaking in Latino Communities*. Milton Park, Abingdon: Routledge.

Rodriguez, R. 2005. "The Foundational Process of Cities in Spanish America: The Law of the Indies as a Planning Tool for Urbanization in Early Colonial Towns in Venezuela." *Focus* 2 (1): 47–58.

Rogers, O., and R. Strange. 2015. "Indiana Population Projections." *InContext*. http://www.incontext.indiana.edu/2008/sept-oct/1.asp.

Rojas, J. 1991. "The Enchanted Environment: The Creation of Place by Mexicans and Mexican-Americans in East Los Angeles." Master's thesis, Massachusetts Institute of Technology.

Romero Gonzalez, E., and R. P. Lejano. 2009. "New Urbanism and the Barrio." *Environment and Planning* 41 (12): 2946–63.

Saenz, R. 2010. *Population Bulletin Update: Latinos in the United States 2010*. Washington, D.C.: Population Reference Bureau.

Sampson, R. J. 2012. *Great American City: Chicago and the Enduring Neighborhood Effect*. Chicago: University of Chicago Press.

Sandoval, G. 2010. *Immigrants and the Revitalization of Los Angeles: Development and Change in MacArthur Park*. Amherst, N.Y.: Cambria Press.

Sandoval, G., and M. Maldonado. 2012. "Latino Urbanism Revisited: Placemaking in New Gateways and the Urban-Rural Interface." *Journal of Urbanism: International Research on Placemaking and Urban Sustainability* 5 (2–3): 193–218.

Shaftoe, H. 2008. *Convivial Urban Spaces: Creating Effective Public Places*. London: Earthscan in association with the International Institute for Environment and Development.

Singer, A., S. W. Hardwick, and C. Brettell. 2008. *Twenty-First Century Gateways: Immigrant Incorporation in Suburban America.* Washington, D.C.: Brookings Institution Press.

Smith, H. A., and O. J. Furuseth. 2006. *Latinos in the New South: Transformations of Place.* Aldershot, UK: Ashgate.

Snodgrass, M. 2008. "Bienvenidos a Talapolis: How a Small Town in Mexico Came to Call Indianapolis Home." *Nuvo,* November 24. https://www.nuvo.net/news/news/bienvenidos-a-talapolis/article_7947db03-3790-5db7-81ed-e88626a8089c.html.

Sorkin, M. 1992. *Variations on a Theme Park: The New American City and the End of Public Space.* New York: Noonday Press.

Sports, J. 1998. "In Search of Belonging: The Hispanic Religious Presence in Indianapolis." *Polis Center Newsletter,* Fall. http://www.polis.iupui.edu/RUC/Newsletters/Religion/vol4no1.htm.

Stephens, J. 2008. "Out of the Enclave: Latinos Adapt, and Adapt to, the American City." *Planetizen,* September 22. https://www.planetizen.com/node/35091.

Sucher, D. 2003. *City Comforts: How to Build an Urban Village.* Seattle: City Comforts.

Suro, R. 2002. *Latino Growth in Metropolitan America: Changing Patterns, New Locations.* Brookings, July 1. https://www.brookings.edu/research/latino-growth-in-metropolitan-america-changing-patterns-new-locations/.

Sutton, S. 2010. "Rethinking Commercial Revitalization: A Neighborhood Small Business Perspective." *Economic Development Quarterly* 24 (4): 352–71.

Taylor, P., A. Gonzalez-Barrera, J. Passel, and M. Lopez. 2012. "An Awakened Giant: The Hispanic Electorate Is Likely to Double by 2030." Pew Research Center, November 14. http://www.pewhispanic.org/2012/11/14/an-awakened-giant-the-hispanic-electorate-is-likely-to-double-by-2030/.

Thorp, E. 2004. "Immigration and Urban Revitalization in Philadelphia: Immigrant Entrepreneurship and Improving Opportunity in the Local Economy." Philadelphia: Welcoming Center for New Pennsylvanians. http://courses.temple.edu/neighbor/world/revitalization.pdf.

Tornoe, J. 2004. "Supermarkets: The Latino Influence." *Hispanic Trending,* October 15. http://juantornoe.blogs.com/hispanictrending/2004/10/supermarkets_th.html.

Touraine, A. 1988. *Return of the Actor: Social Theory in Postindustrial Society.* Minneapolis: University of Minnesota Press.

Trabalzi, F., and G. Sandoval. 2010. "The Exotic Other: Latinos and the Remaking of Community Identity in Perry, Iowa." *Community Development* 41 (1).

Tuan, Y. 1977. *Space and Place: The Perspective of Experience.* Minneapolis: University of Minnesota Press.

ULI (Urban Land Institute). 2013. *A ULI Advisory Services Panel Report: Southwest Detroit Michigan.* http://uli.org/wp-content/uploads/ULI-Documents/Detroit_PanelReport_v4_lowres-with-cover.pdf.

U.S. Census Bureau. 2011. *The Hispanic Population 2010.* May. https://www.census.gov/prod/cen2010/briefs/c2010br-04.pdf.

U.S. Department of Labor. 2012. *The Latino Labor Force at a Glance.* April 5. https://www.dol.gov/_sec/media/reports/HispanicLaborForce/HispanicLaborForce.pdf.

Valle, V., and R. Torres. 2000. *Latino Metropolis.* Minneapolis: University of Minnesota Press.

Vargas, Z. 1999. *Proletarians of the North: A History of Mexican Industrial Workers in Detroit and the Midwest, 1917–1933.* Berkeley: University of California Press.

Vergara, C., G. Leclerc, M. J. Dear, and D. Dishman. 2000. *El Nuevo Mundo: The Landscape of Latino Los Angeles.* Los Angeles: Southern California Studies Center, University of Southern California.

Wheeler, S. M., and T. Beatley. 2015. *The Sustainable Urban Development Reader*. Johanneshov: MTM.

Wilson, H., and A. Singer. 2011. *Immigrants in 2010 Metropolitan America: A Decade of Change*. Washington, D.C.: Brookings Institution.

Winnick, L. 1990. *New People in Old Neighborhoods: The Role of New Immigrants in Rejuvenating New York's Communities*. New York: Russell Sage Foundation.

Yin, R. K. 1994. *Case Study Research: Design and Methods*. Thousand Oaks, Calif.: Sage Publications.

Zambrana, R. E. 1995. *Understanding Latino Families: Scholarship, Policy, and Practice*. Thousand Oaks, Calif.: Sage Publications.

Zapata, M. 2012. "Planning for Possible Futures: The Role of Scenario Planning in Cross-Cultural Deliberation." In *Diálogos: Placemaking in Latino Communities*, edited by M. Rios, L. Vazquez, and L. Miranda. Milton Park, Abingdon: Routledge.

Zelinsky, W., and B. A. Lee. 1998. "Heterolocalism: An Alternative Model of the Sociospatial Behaviour of Immigrant Ethnic Communities." *International Journal of Population Geography* 4 (4): 281–98.

Zúñiga, V., and R. Hernández-León. 2005. *New Destinations: Mexican Immigration in the United States*. New York: Russell Sage Foundation.

INDEX

accessibility: of McDowell Corridor, 65–66; of West Vernor-Bagley Street Corridor, 80; of West Washington Street Corridor, 107

adaptation, 73; of cities, 39; development through, 84; of Latino immigrant communities, 51; in Morse Road Corridor and Sullivan Avenue, 94, 98; in West Washington Street Corridor, 108

advertising, 17–18; color use in, 45; of storefronts, 45–46

age, 11; in Arizona, 69–70; in electoral power, 25, 27

American dream, 23

American FactFinder (Census Bureau, U.S.), 9, 16

Americas Society (Council of the Americas), 111

appropriation, 34; in Latino urbanism, 57; reappropriation and, 47

architecture: examples of, 134; local culture expressed by, 133–34; in shared spaces, 140

Arizona: age in, 69–70; white population in, 68–69. *See also* McDowell Corridor, Phoenix, Arizona; Phoenix, Arizona

Aronson, David, 18

assimilation, 51

attractions: ethnic entrepreneurship celebrated through, 127–32; examples of, 129; joint ventures in, 130; urban planning of, 128

Ballard, Greg, 112

biophilia, 58; cultural significance of, 61–63

birth rates, 16

brand names, 22

Bureau of Economic Analysis, U.S., 72

buying patterns, 21

capacity building, 80; in McDowell Corridor, 66; of Morse Road Corridor and Sullivan Avenue, 92–93; urban planning and, 132–33; of West Washington Street Corridor, 107

Card, David, 56

Carnegie Endowment for International Peace, 18

case study: on economic reinterpretation of place, 37; examination of, 62–63; findings from, 116–23; of McDowell Corridor, 63–76; of Morse Road Corridor and Sullivan Avenue, 90–105; in reclaimed and readapted spaces, 36; significance of, 3–4; summary of, 120–21; transformation in, 62; on West Vernor-Bagley Street, 76–89; of West Washington Street Corridor, 105–16

Catholic Church, 84

Census Bureau, U.S.: on age, 11; *American FactFinder* from, 9, 16; on ethnicity, 11; on Indianapolis, Indiana, 111; on minorities, 59; on Ohio, 95; Survey of Business Owners from, 95

Census Bureau Survey of Business Owners, U.S., 24–25

Center for Competitiveness and Prosperity Research, 67

cities: adaptability of, 39; blocks of, 5; character of, 40–41; cognitive mapping of, 31; decentralization to despatialization of, 40; planning efforts in, 124–25; public spaces in, 40–41; re-urbanizing of, 8; Sucher on buildings in, 42–43

cognitive mapping, 31

Columbus, Ohio: Latino population in, 95–96. *See also* Morse Road Corridor and Sullivan Avenue, Columbus, Ohio

Francis, Marc, 4
future planning: implications for, 124–
27; of McDowell Corridor, 72–76; for
Morse Road Corridor and Sullivan
Avenue, 102–5; in West Vernor-Bagley Street Corridor, 85–89; for West
Washington Street Corridor, 112–15

GDP. *See* gross domestic product
gender, 22
gentrification, 33
geographical distribution: of Latino businesses, 20; of Latino population, 11–13
geographic distribution: of electoral
power, 25–26
Google aerial maps, 116
grocery stores, 19–20
gross domestic product (GDP), 16

The Harvard Business Review, 21
Hispanic population, 14–15

immigrant businesses, 4; entrepreneurs
of, 19, 72–73; revitalization through,
119; significance of, 143
"Immigrant Entrepreneurs" (Aronson), 18
immigrant neighborhoods: culture in,
32–33; economic revitalization in, 5
immigration: as economic strength,
44; of Latino population, 10–11; settlement patterns in, 59; urban environments shaped by, 10–11. *See also*
Latino immigrant communities
income, 122–23
Indiana: Latino population growth in,
109–10. *See also* West Washington
Street Corridor, Indianapolis, Indiana
Indiana Business Research Center of the
Indiana University Kelley School of
Business, 109
Indianapolis, Indiana: Census Bureau,
U.S., on, 111; Latino businesses in,
112; suburbs of, 105; visual aspects of,
113–14. *See also* West Washington
Street Corridor, Indianapolis, Indiana
Indiana University Kelley School of
Business, 109

informal interviews: on entrepreneurship, 118; questions for, 6; with
shop-owners, 47. *See also* case study
infrastructure, 58
innovation, 4
Institute for Taxation and Economic
Policy (ITEP), 112
Internet, 59
Islamic law, 105
ITEP. *See* Institute for Taxation and Economic Policy

Jacobs, Allan, 32

labor camps, 48–49
labor force, 23–27
landscape architects, 6
LASED. *See* Latin Americans for Social
and Economic Development
Las Vegas Sun, 72
Latin Americans for Social and Economic Development (LASED), 84, 86
Latino Americans. *See specific topics*
Latino businesses, 8; comfort from,
61; commerce in, 61; geographical
distribution of, 20; in Indianapolis,
Indiana, 112; markets as, 118; reasons
for, 117; receipts from, 9–10; Spanish
language in, 20; in West Washington
Street Corridor, 115
Latino immigrant communities, 7–8;
adaptation of, 51; assimilation of, 51;
cultural impact of, 45
Latino market, 13–20
Latino neighborhoods: placemaking
effects on, 7, 38–49; revitalization of,
18–19; structure of, 39–49
Latino population: buying patterns of,
21; change of, 27–28; in Columbus,
Ohio, 95–96; contributions of, 9; by
county, 14–15; in Detroit, Michigan,
77–78; ethnic plurality of, 15–16;
food of, 47; geographical distribution of, 11–13; growth factors for,
7, 9, 15–16; immigration of, 10–11;
impact documentation of, 124; in
Indiana, 109–10; as largest minority,

13; neighborhood revitalization by, 18–19; percentage change in, 14–15; purchasing power of, 20–23; resource stress from, 10; shifting demographics from growth of, 10–12; stereotypes of, 21; unemployment rate of, 24; in West Washington Street Corridor, 110

Latino urbanism, 7–8; appropriation in, 57; contested space in, 36–37; in everyday, 35–36; focus points for, 34–38; literature on, 33–38; participatory and inclusionary approaches to, 37; placemaking in, 29; planning of, 44; as predating smart growth, 58; in reclaimed and readapted spaces, 36; revitalization as transformation of, 122; sustainable urbanism and, 57–58; theoretical framework for, 57

Leadership in Energy and Environmental Design (LEED), 58

lifestyle, 35

Local Initiatives Support Corporation (LISC), 114

Loukaitou-Sideris, A., 51

Lynch, Kevin, 31

markets, 118

Martin Prosperity Institute, 99

McDowell Corridor, Phoenix, Arizona: accessibility of, 65–66; age in, 70; business types in, 75; capacity building in, 66; case study of, 63–76; characteristics of, 64; commercial nodes in, 74; context of, 63–65; demographic trends and impacts in, 67–71; density in, 65; economic trends in, 71–72; growth of, 65; local conditions in, 65–67; location of, 64; retail in, 66; safety in, 66; shopping centers in, 64–65; threshold elements in, 65–67; vernacular expressions in, 67

Medicare, 111–12

Mexicans and Mexican Americans, 80–81

Mexicantown Baker, 86

Michigan. *See* West Vernor-Bagley Street Corridor, Detroit, Michigan

La Michoacana Tortilla Factory, 86

Midwest, U.S., 13

minorities, 59

Morse Road Corridor and Sullivan Avenue, Columbus, Ohio: adaptive use examples in, 94, 98; business rankings in, 99–101; capacity building of, 92–93; case study of, 90–105; community centers in, 102; context of, 90–91; demographic trends in, 93–95; density of, 91–93; economic trends in, 96–102; food in, 101–2; future planning for, 102–5; immigrant community in, 104; local conditions of, 91–93; multiethnic shopping plazas in, 103; physical space of, 90; retail of, 92–93; safety in, 92–93; threshold elements of, 91–93

multiethnic shopping plazas, 103

National Highway System, 106

NERA Economic Consulting, 23

New Urbanism, 39

Nielsen Company, 16

Obama, Barack, 27

Ohio: Census Bureau, U.S., on, 95. *See also* Columbus, Ohio; Morse Road Corridor and Sullivan Avenue, Columbus, Ohio

Ohio State University, 6, 95

Oldenburg, Ray, 51–52

Ong, P. M., 51

open-air culture: corridors in, 47–49; food in, 48; streetscapes in, 47–48. *See also* biophilia

party affiliation, 26–27

Pew Hispanic Center: on electoral power, 25–26; on 2016 political impact, 25–26

Pew Research Center, 9; on public transit, 60–61

Phoenix, Arizona: commercial corridors in, 68. *See also* McDowell Corridor, Phoenix, Arizona

ABOUT THE AUTHOR

JESUS J. LARA is an associate professor and Master's Program chair in the Knowlton School's City and Regional Planning Section at the Ohio State University. His research interests include sustainable urban design, Latino urbanism, community development, and sociocultural factors in community design. He is the author of *Placemaking in 21st-Century American Cities* (Taylor and Francis Group, 2012) and is the co-editor of and contributor to *Remaking Metropolis: Global Challenges of the Urban Landscape* (Routledge, 2012). He earned his PhD in environmental design and planning from Arizona State University in 2006.